UNTO THY SEED

WILL I GIVE THIS LAND.

GENESIS 12:7

God's promise to Abraham, patriarch of Judaism,

Christianity, and Islam

CRADLE & CRUCIBLE

CRADLE & CRUCIBLE

HISTORY AND FAITH IN THE MIDDLE EAST

INTRODUCTION BY DANIEL SCHORR

WITH DAVID FROMKIN, ZAHI HAWASS,

YOSSI KLEIN HALEVI, SANDRA MACKEY,

CHARLES M. SENNOTT, MILTON VIORST,

AND ANDREW WHEATCROFT

NATIONAL GEOGRAPHIC

WASHINGTON, D.C.

*Christian children display a homemade cross in Jerusalem,
where religion often determines fate.*

CONTENTS

In Gaza, a young Arab woman holds what could be a symbol of peace in a land of continual strife. For almost 4,000 years this vulnerable place has had countless masters— from the Philistines to Alexander, from the Arabs to the Israelis.

INTRODUCTION

DANIEL SCHORR

I AM BOTH HONORED AND PUZZLED TO HAVE BEEN INVITED by National Geographic to write an introduction to this impressive survey of the Middle East. Honored because of the scholarship that I become associated with. Puzzled because I come nowhere near sharing the depth of that scholarship. Perhaps my contribution comes from my age. While lacking specialized knowledge of this tormented region of the world, I did live through some of its torments.

I knew about the Middle East before it was the "Middle East." I grew up calling it the "Near East" because that was the way it looked from Britain—the Western power in charge when the region was being divided up after the collapse of the Ottoman Empire. "Far East" was Asia, and "Middle East" was the in-between portion around Iran and Iraq.

I first set foot in the Middle (or Near) East under unusual circumstances. On May 15, 1948, working as a correspondent in the Netherlands, I boarded a KLM Constellation airliner to cover the nationalist insurrection in the Netherlands Indies (now Indonesia). As evening fell, the plane approached Cairo's King Farouk Airport for a planned overnight stop.

Coming over Port Said and the Suez Canal, we saw searchlights crisscrossing the sky and pinpointing our plane. We landed to be met by excited Egyptian Army officers, who advised that we had violated the wartime ban on night landings. Wartime? The war against Israel had started while we were in the air.

Hoping to utilize the unexpected opportunity to convey some of the color of Cairo at war, I tried to take a taxi into town but was told that, because of the war, passengers were restricted to the airport. Trying to send a cable to my New York editor to describe what I could, I was told that telegrams now had to go through wartime censorship, but the censor had not yet been appointed.

A first frustrating encounter with a part of the world that was my ancestral home. More than a half century later, I have still not been much in the Middle East, but I am spiritually of the Middle East.

BORN IN 1916, A YEAR BEFORE Britain's Balfour Declaration promised a "national home for the Jewish people" in Palestine, I was nurtured on that promise. My widowed mother, a devoted Zionist, was a leading member of Bronx District 13 of the Zionist Organization of America. Her brother, Naftali, had been one of the early chalutzim (pioneers) who had left Eastern Europe to settle in Palestine. Eventually, he came to New York to live with us, a much admired member of the family.

At my mother's gentle instigation, I went five afternoons a week to Talmud Torah (Hebrew school) and became fluent in the language, even to being able to write Hebrew poetry—faculties I lost later in life. My enthusiasm was not for religion but for Zionism. In DeWitt Clinton High School I was president of the Hebrew Society. In City College, I clashed with the Communists because they were anti-Zionist. (Ironically, being known as anti-Communist at City College in the 1930s may have actually saved me from some later red-baiting.)

My Bible study introduced me to Middle East landmarks I had never seen. Embedded in my mental geography were Mount Ararat, where Noah's ark came to rest, and Mount Sinai, which Moses ascended to receive the Ten Commandments. I was figuratively with Joshua at the walls of Jericho. On my mental map, Babylon meant Galut (exile).

Involved in Zionist youth activities, I met visiting dignitaries from Palestine. One of those was David Ben-Gurion, destined to be Israel's first prime minister. He spoke ardently of *aliyah,* which means immigration, or, more literally, a going up or return. He emphasized that Jewish security in Palestine required an influx from the Diaspora. He told us that it was the duty of American Jews to return to Zion. Few of us were ready for that.

But we were otherwise willing to be supportive. As a teenager I carried a coin collection box for the Jewish National Fund, which bought land for settlement in Palestine. As early as 1929 I participated in demonstrations against Britain, the mandatory power, for seeking to limit Jewish immigration and failing to curb Arab violence against Jews.

Jews shared with Muslims and Christians an attachment to Palestine, but the Jewish attachment acquired a new dimension with Hitler and the Holocaust. For hundreds of thousands of European Jews Palestine became not sentiment but salvation.

For this drama I had a professional vantage point. In 1937, still in college, I got a job as assistant editor of the Jewish Telegraphic Agency. That permitted me to observe how differences between Zionists and non-Zionists in the Jewish Agency for Palestine faded away in the struggle to keep Palestine open to European Jews, many of whom had converted to Zionism in reaction to Hitler's actions.

I met some of the men of the underground Haganah, the burgeoning Jewish Army in Palestine. Some of the same men who fought under British command against the German Army in North Africa also formed a secret corps that smuggled Jewish refugees onto the beaches near Haifa. From them I learned the term "Aliyah Bet" ("Aliyah B"), the illegal immigration movement. I wrote of the strenuous efforts of the British military to curb the Jewish influx in the interest of staying on good terms with the Arabs.

I wrote of the British commission reports that tried to control Jewish immigration. In 1939 a British white paper proposed dividing Palestine into an Arab state and a small Jewish state—the first effort at partition, and not to be the last. The Jews rejected the proposal, but so did the Arabs.

The sense of Palestine as the scene of intractable conflict was deepened by the pressure of Jewish flight from annihilation in Europe. Once the war was over, Britain was ready to give up its frustrating Palestine mandate. In 1948 the United Nations, successor to the League of Nations, created the states of Israel and Transjordan. There followed a five-nation Arab assault aimed at strangling the infant Jewish state in its cradle.

By then I was no longer deeply involved in the Middle East. After Pearl Harbor I had been drafted into the U. S. Army. After the war, seeking to expand my professional horizons beyond Jewish journalism, I had gone to the Netherlands as a freelance correspondent for the *Christian Science Monitor* and *Time* magazine. Thus it was that, on May 15, 1948, I landed in Cairo to learn that Arab forces were marching on the newly created Jewish state.

But the Middle East continued recurrently to come across my radar screen. In 1953 I joined CBS News in Washington as diplomatic correspondent. It was at a time when a new chapter was opening in the tumultuous history of the Middle East. Once an arena for ethnic strife and colonial intrigue, the region now became an arena in the developing East-West Cold War. Egypt's charismatic leader, Gamal Abdel Nasser, opened the area to Soviet penetration and recognized Communist China.

At the State Department I observed Secretary John Foster Dulles waging the Eisenhower Administration's campaign to undermine Nasser, withdrawing promised support for the massive project to build a high dam at Aswan. The Eisenhower Administration also tried its hand, unsuccessfully, in mediating the Arab-Israeli standoff. But the administration was really more concerned with trying to shut the Soviet Union out of the Middle East.

In 1955 CBS sent me to open a news bureau in Moscow, which the post-Stalin thaw had made possible. It was a period when Soviet propaganda was going all out to sharpen tensions over the Middle East, perhaps to divert attention from the anti-Communist stirrings in the Soviet backyard in Poland and Hungary. I happened to be with the American ambassador Charles "Chip" Bohlen on October 29, 1956, when word came that Israel, Britain, and France had launched an attack on the Sinai to block Nasser's nationalization of the Suez Canal.

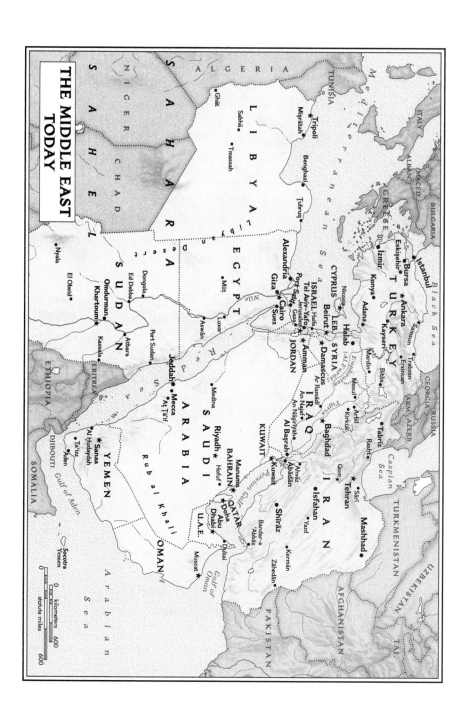

THE MIDDLE EAST TODAY

Shaking his head mournfully, Bohlen said, "This is a terrible tragedy. This will enable Khrushchev to divert attention from his bloodbath in Hungary." And, indeed, Premier Nikita Khrushchev moved swiftly to focus world attention on Suez. He threatened Soviet intervention in the conflict, and the Kremlin announced that 125,000 Soviet "volunteers" were ready to go to Egypt. This was largely hype, but it had its effect. I visited the Egyptian Embassy in Moscow and found no one lining up to sign the "volunteers' register." (The Soviet censor would not permit me to report that fact in my radio broadcast.)

American pressure more than Soviet threats forced an end to the Suez invasion. In an effort to show strength in the region, the President promulgated an "Eisenhower Doctrine," which authorized the use of American forces if necessary to avoid "a vacuum in the Middle East."

The Eisenhower Doctrine followed me to my next assignment. Barred from the Soviet Union at the end of 1957, I was stationed at the United Nations. On July 14, 1958, in response to nationalist convulsions in Iraq, Jordan, and Lebanon, the Sixth Fleet assembled in the Mediterranean and put ashore some 9,000 U.S. Marines in Lebanon. Secretary Dulles said the United States was acting to counter a Soviet threat to wrest the Middle East from the free world. The UN Security Council was called into emergency session, and CBS assigned me to anchor three days of live coverage of a session that quickly bogged down in procedural debate.

Since the ineffectual Eisenhower Doctrine, I have watched a succession of Presidents no more successful in designing doctrines to still the Middle East maelstrom. As reporter and commentator for CBS, CNN, and National Public Radio successively, I have watched the on-again, off-again peace efforts, and I have encountered the Arab and Israeli principals as they came through Washington, each seeking the support of a mainly baffled superpower.

The Middle East remains the oldest established crisis in the world. One is tempted to say, with the French, that the more things change, the more they remain the same.

But there has been one profound change—the advent of the suicide bomber, perhaps the ultimate asymmetric weapon. On Prime Minister Yitzhak Rabin's last visit to Washington in 1995, I asked him what the answer was to the suicide bomber, then still a relative rarity.

"We have no answer to the suicide bomber," he said slowly. "We can answer many kinds of threat, but not the suicide bomber."

The Middle East remains the region that for years—centuries—has shown a capacity like no other to affect the destiny of the world. It is why I think the National Geographic is performing a great service in offering this illuminating study.

Inscrutable figures found at Ain Ghazal, near Amman, Jordan, date from 6500 B.C. and are counted among the earliest realistic likenesses of human beings ever discovered. Well-formed features, as recognizable as our own, show a high level of artistry.

CHAPTER ONE

8500 TO 300 B.C.

RISE AND FALL

A CIVILIZED PREHISTORY

ZAHI HAWASS

THE ANCIENT NEAR EAST—THE AREA SWEEPING FROM THE northeast corner of Africa up through the Arabian Peninsula and on to the southwest part of Asia—was the cradle of human civilization. The aptly named Fertile Crescent provided its inhabitants with rivers such as the Nile, the Jordan, and the Tigris-Euphrates, as well as rich soils, useful raw materials, and a hospitable climate. The meshing of these elements helped engender the rise of civilization by both allowing and forcing humans to find new ways of manipulating their environment. It was here that groups of hunter-gatherers first learned to domesticate wild plants and animals, and a growing population of farmers began to settle into small villages. Soon towns grew into cities and then into centralized city-states and nations. Eventually, some of these nations expanded into great empires, whose fortunes waxed and waned over the centuries.

The transition from hunter-gatherer to farmer was a gradual one, taking place over thousands of years, with different areas within the larger region developing at different rates. Distinct local cultures arose and changed over time, but certain basic similarities were found throughout the Near East. In general, dwellings were simple and housed single families. Social organization was basically egalitarian and based on kinship ties. Religion and art were inseparable and seemingly focused on fertility. Archaeological evidence for this period is complex and in many cases indirect, and scholarly understanding of cultural developments here is still in the process of changing and becoming more nuanced as more data become available.

During the period directly preceding the appearance of agriculture, the ancient Near East was inhabited by small groups who lived off the land. As the glaciers of the last ice age began to recede, around 10,000 B.C., the warming climate increased the local food supply. The richness and predictability of natural resources—wild cereals to harvest in the spring, nuts to gather in the fall, and an abundance of wild but easily hunted game such as gazelle—allowed the population to increase and become more sedentary. Permanent settlements of foragers appeared in the region of Canaan (modern Israel) during the tenth and ninth millennia B.C. The largest of these villages housed several hundred inhabitants and included semi-subterranean houses and storage pits to hold surplus foods. By 8500 B.C. such artifacts as seashells and stone bowls found in some burials are evidence of social ranking in the form of special grave goods.

During the ninth millennium the region experienced a cycle of drought. Population density had already reached the point where it was no longer an easy task simply to move groups to new areas when local resources had been exhausted. Much of the process of domestication of wild plants may have been a reaction to the sudden need for a more reliable food supply to keep up with an expanded population.

Once the concept of domesticating plants had been recognized and applied, it may have taken only a century or two for wild grains to be replaced by cultivated ones. At the site of Abu Hureyra in Syria, the remains of wild grains, nuts, and the bones of wild gazelles were found in one level; in the next, dated to around 8000 B.C., domesticated grains appeared. Soon afterward, the inhabitants learned to herd sheep and goats. By about 7000 B.C. there were signs of early agriculture in Canaan, Anatolia (modern Turkey), and what is now western Iran and Iraqi Kurdistan. These are found mainly at sites located near lakeshores and rivers, areas ideal for the cultivation of cereals. The spread of this new technology was uneven: On the southern Anatolian plateau, for example, the inhabitants of Suberde continued to focus on hunting, while their neighbors at Hacilar, only 120 miles away, were already farming.

Agriculture was slow to appear in the Nile Valley. During the arid phase after 8500 B.C., people seem to have migrated between the Nile Valley and the increasingly dry savanna lands to the east and west, bringing herds of partially domesticated cattle with them. Farming did not become an important way of life in Egypt until the sixth millennium B.C.

The first farming villages in the Near East had populations ranging from the hundreds into the low thousands. The basic social unit remained the family, and relationships were organized around kinship and principles of reciprocity. In such circumstances disputes would have been arbitrated, trade for foreign goods controlled, group security ensured, and surpluses redistributed by particularly charismatic and competent individuals. Skulls covered with plaster and inlaid with shell eyes from a number of sites have been interpreted as evidence of a widespread ancestor cult, perhaps featuring such leaders. The power held by these people would not have been hereditary at first, but later it would have been passed to the next generation, along with important economic benefits such as ownership of land or grazing rights.

Analogies with historically documented societies as well as forensic studies of the bones from at least one site suggest a gender-based division of labor. Women took the lead in agricultural activities and are believed to have domesticated grain. Men probably continued to hunt some wild game and tended to the herding of domesticated flocks. As surpluses became more reliable, talented artisans could be supported so that they could practice their crafts full-time. Over time, this created a new class of people.

Architectural styles varied from site to site: One village might have simple round or oval semisubterranean houses with domed roofs arranged in clusters; another might have rectangular, multiroomed houses with built-in ovens and storage basins arranged around courtyards and narrow streets. In general, dwellings continued to be relatively small, for single families at most, and floors were often plastered and painted red. Some groups built such communal structures as granaries and threshing floors.

At Jericho, in the Jordan Valley, a large settlement of beehive-shaped houses was surrounded by a massive stone wall, complete with towers and an encircling ditch, by about 7500 B.C. This may have been either for protection from flooding or as a defense against neighboring populations. The large Anatolian village of Çatal Hüyük (circa 6300–5500 B.C.) is unique, with rectangular buildings of mud brick packed together so closely that the only access was through ladders from the roofs. Each family group lived in a large room outfitted with plastered clay niches, benches, and ovens, with one or more storerooms attached.

Stone, especially flint, was the principal material for tools during this period, and this lithic technology was extremely advanced. The most important new invention was pottery—hard-baked clay vessels used for transporting and storing food and water. Each culture developed its own shapes and decorative features. Changes in pottery styles over time give archaeologists important clues to relative dating, while finds of imported pottery and the spread of distinctive features provide crucial evidence of intercultural contact. Another technology that developed during this period was metalworking, used to fashion small pins and pendants.

Early agricultural societies were extremely dependent on the proper and predictable functioning of the natural world. The guarantee of fertility, which ensures that there will be enough food to go around, was the basic focus for the religion of this time. Both human and animal figurines of clay or stone have been found at most village sites. Most of these, especially images of abundantly fleshed females—prototypes for the great mother goddess seen in later cultures around the region—are thought to have cultic significance connected with fertility or sexuality.

Monumental human figures of plaster have been found in several places. Various scholars have suggested that they are portrayals of gods and goddesses, representations of revered ancestors, or even figures of ghosts. But whatever they were meant to embody, they would have been used as important symbols in cultic ceremonies.

Cult buildings have been found for the early agricultural period at only a few sites. At Çatal Hüyük almost a third of the large rooms had been turned into shrines, with elaborate wall paintings depicting such themes as women giving birth to animals and reliefs incorporating the horns of various animals, especially cattle, thought to be part of a cattle cult.

Cult or ritual sites have been found at 'Ain Ghazal, in what is now Jordan, at Jericho, and in several other locations. Later in this period, as populations grew and societies became more complex, cult buildings were more common. In these later times, temples often functioned as the focal point for towns.

Burial practices during the same period provide evidence for a widespread belief in an afterlife. Bodies are curled on their sides in simple pits, usually found within settlements. Some graves contain goods such as tools, pots, or jewelry. Certain cultures appear to have removed the heads, left the bodies out until the flesh was gone (graphically depicted in a wall painting at Çatal Hüyük of vultures devouring headless corpses), and then buried the disarticulated skeletons. Separate cemeteries are found only in Egypt, in the low desert bordering the Nile floodplain. Far fewer burials are found at almost all sites than would be expected from settlement sizes, and it may be that only certain people were given elaborate burials.

By the sixth millennium B.C., the many distinct cultures in the region were connected to one another through a large trading network. Stone for tools was an important raw material, and obsidian from Anatolia and Armenia is found as far away as Jericho and the lower Euphrates Valley. Luxury goods such as seashells are found far inland. The entrepreneurs responsible for the movement of such goods also transferred cultural innovations from one area to another.

THE INVENTION OF AGRICULTURE was a watershed in human history. The ability of people to build permanent settlements allowed cultures to accumulate wealth and develop concepts such as ownership of land and possessions. The enormous population growth that accompanied the domestication of plants and animals soon reached the tipping point, after which there was no returning to earlier patterns of hunting and gathering. The interplay of human and environmental factors caused a rise in social complexity, leading to an irreversible transformation of the ancient world.

Gradually, settlements became larger and more complex, and new technologies, from weaving to irrigation, developed. As food surpluses became more reliable, they could be used to support full-time craftspeople and a growing class of elites responsible for managing the redistribution of surplus goods, overseeing trade, and ensuring the security of the population. At some point nomadic animal herding became a specialized activity, and a new class of pastoralists arose on the edges of the agricultural society. New patterns of inheritance concentrated wealth and power in the hands of the few. These developments interacted in a complex dance, setting the stage for the appearance of "civilization."

THE THRESHOLD OF CIVILIZATION WAS CROSSED first during the late fourth millennium B.C. in Mesopotamia and Egypt, and this new way of life soon spread throughout the region. The various civilizations that arose in the Near East over the next thousand years were different in significant ways, but they shared certain features. The populations were clustered in urban centers, often focused around a temple. Some cities commanded large hinterlands and acted as city-states. In some areas, towns and cities became unified as nation-states. The societies were stratified and political organization was complex, with a small ruling elite headed by a king, a class of administrators and priests, a layer of artists and craftsmen, and, at the bottom, the mass of farmers, fisherpeople, herders, and slaves. The innovation of writing appeared, and art reached high levels of achievement. Religion became complex and primarily state-run. Monumental architecture appeared, and funerary practices became elaborate and highly stratified. An immense and complex trading network evolved, and war became an essential tool of international relations.

The beginnings of urbanism can be traced in the Mesopotamian temple-town of Eridu, in what is now southern Iraq, settled by 5500 B.C. In the earlier levels there is no evidence for social stratification, but by 4500 B.C. an elite class lived in substantial homes around a central temple, craftsmen and their families lived in smaller dwellings nearby, and farming families lived outside the central settlement in simple houses.

During the next thousand years, the first urban centers developed from these temple-towns. By 3500 B.C. the Mesopotamian city of Uruk consisted of 617 acres of closely packed houses around a temple complex. The villages for at least six miles around were dependent on the city and formed part of its economic base. Similar situations existed in neighboring cities.

The desire for security and access to greater resources led early cities such as Uruk to expand their spheres of influence. By about 3100 B.C. the Sumerians, with their capital at Ur, held sway over the lower Mesopotamian region. Ur's fortified walls (evidence that war was becoming an important political and economic tool) enclosed about 240 acres, with a population of approximately 24,000. Inside were temples, palaces, and administrative offices; outside were fields and the houses of the people who worked them. City-states were also developing elsewhere in Mesopotamia, along the eastern Mediterranean coast, and in Syria, Anatolia, and Iran, and petty wars were frequent and bloody.

In other regions geography encouraged the emergence of nation-states. By 3000 B.C. Egypt had established a united kingdom reaching from the Nile Delta in the north to the First Cataract (just south of Aswan) in the south. This unification was a gradual process: The archaeological record shows that cultural groups from the south gradually absorbed their northern neighbors. The official political history of Egypt, reconstructed through royally inscribed and dated artifacts as well as later annals and king lists, begins at the dawn of the third millennium. To the northeast, in the southwestern highlands of present-day Iran, another kingdom, Elam, emerged about 2500 B.C. and remained viable for almost a thousand years.

Early urbanized society in the Near East was highly centralized and highly stratified, with power and wealth concentrated in the hands of the elite. At the top of the economic and political pyramid was the king. In Sumeria, the high priest of the temple at first also served as secular ruler of the city-state. Later, as warfare with neighboring cities and states gained in importance, military leaders took over secular control and ruled as kings. The Sumerian monarch was said to be appointed by the gods, and kingship was through merit rather than birth. In Egypt the king stood at the head of a vast bureaucracy and also acted as head of the state religion. He was considered a living god, and his chief queen was the incarnation of a goddess. Right to rule was hereditary, passed from father to son or sometimes from brother to brother.

The ruling class gained the ability to wield enormous coercive power. The people at the bottom of the heap could either be encouraged (with religion playing a major role) or forced to build monumental temples,

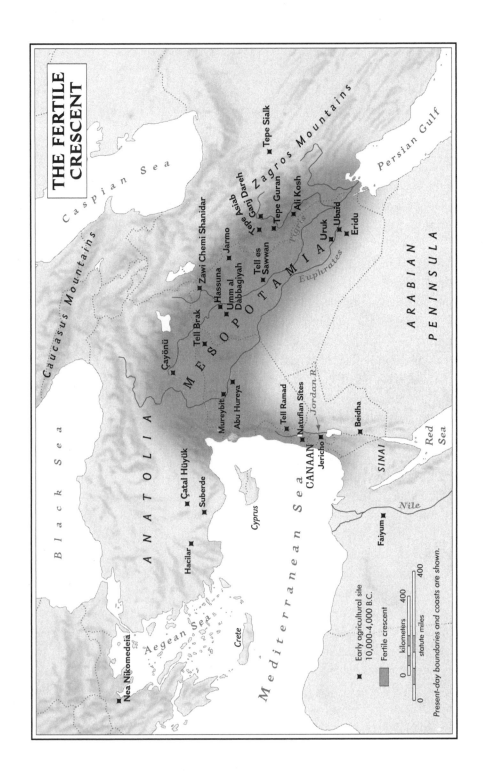

THE FERTILE CRESCENT

Persian Gulf

Caspian Sea

Caspian Sea

Zagros Mountains

Tepe Sialk

Caucasus Mountains

Ganj Dareh

Tepe Asiab

Zawi Chemi Shanidar

Ali Kosh

Tepe Guran

Eridu

Hassuna

Jarmo

Ubaid

Uruk

Umm al
Dabbaghiyah

Tell es
Sawwan

Tigris

Euphrates

Tell Brak

M E S O P O T A M I A

A R A B I A N
P E N I N S U L A

Çayönü

A N A T O L I A

Mureybit

Abu Hureyra

Tell Ramad

Jordan R.

Natufian Sites

Beidha

Red
Sea

Black Sea

Jericho

CANAAN

SINAI

Çatal Hüyük

Suberde

Cyprus

Nile

Faiyum

Hacilar

Mediterranean Sea

Aegean Sea

Crete

Nea Nikomedeia

Early agricultural site
10,000–4,000 B.C.

Fertile crescent

0   kilometers   400

0   statute miles   400

Present-day boundaries and coasts are shown.

palaces, fortifications, and irrigation systems; pay taxes in the form of surpluses; and fight in the army. Early royal tombs at Ur in Mesopotamia and Abydos in Egypt provide evidence for the ultimate coercion in the form of human sacrifice—retainers were killed and buried with their rulers so that they could continue to serve them in the afterlife.

Large administrative and priestly classes arose to keep these complex societies functioning smoothly. Beneath them were artisans who specialized in making pottery, stone vases, or jewelry, and in carving and painting reliefs and sculptures. The majority of the population spent most of their time involved in subsistence activities.

On the fringes of these urban civilizations lived a new class of nomadic pastoralists, groups of people who survived by herding animals. They led their flocks of sheep, goats, or cattle from pasture to pasture, trading milk, skins, wool, and meat to their more settled neighbors. The first biblical patriarch, Abraham, believed to have been born in the Mesopotamian city of Ur, was such a pastoralist.

Artistic achievement took a quantum leap forward during this period. Large-scale stone sculpture appeared and was quickly mastered, metalworking and jewelry making were highly advanced. The royal tombs at Ur contained, among their many treasures, extraordinary sculptures of gilded wood and lapis lazuli and inlaid lyres of surpassing elegance. The Egyp-tians had a great appreciation for beauty and produced astonishing works of art, realized through a combination of pleasing proportions and superb craftsmanship. In the civilized cultures of this time, art served as a symbol of wealth and status. It communicated messages of power and stability, reinforced the existing social structure, and gave each culture its flavor.

As nations and city-states emerged and grew, a vast network of trade evolved. Elite displays of wealth and power became more elaborate, and access to raw materials and luxury goods became increasingly important. States all over the Near East depended on one another for exotic stone and wood, metal ore, resinous gums, and even grain. In most emerging states, the ruling classes kept tight control over trade, organizing expeditions and keeping the profits. The desire for reliable and inexpensive access to important raw materials was a major impetus for territorial expansion, and eventually led to the quest for empire.

As POPULATIONS GREW LARGER and political and economic systems more complex, a recordkeeping system became necessary, so that such things as accounts of surplus goods, land ownership, trade, and calendars could be controlled. Without writing, the administration of these elaborate societies would have become impossibly unwieldy.

The first attempts at recordkeeping were in the form of clay tokens impressed with signs identifying their owners. In Mesopotamia the next step took the form of census or accounting—pictographs of animals accompanied by numbers, incised on tablets of baked clay with pointed reeds. By 3100 B.C. a syllabic system using wedge-shaped (cuneiform) signs, each standing for a consonant-vowel cluster, had developed. First used for the Sumerian language, this kind of writing system was later employed by the speakers of other languages.

A completely distinctive type of writing appeared in Egypt at about the same time. The Egyptian writing system consisted of pictographic signs, each representing one or more consonants or functioning as "determinatives," indications of the type of word they followed. A cursive form of hieroglyphs, called hieratic, was used on papyrus. The first hieroglyphs appear as labels on pottery vessels, ivory tags, and clay sealings, and were soon used to convey historical information.

Within a few centuries Near Eastern writing systems were being used for administrative documents, law codes, letters, and religious, historical, or propagandistic inscriptions. The invention of writing spurred the development of what we call the sciences, although in the ancient conception there was no clear line between science, religion, and magic. These advances were in mathematics, medicine, and astronomy, in which the Sumerians and their successors excelled. Literature began to appear, in many cases formalizing oral traditions but also creating a new art form and new ways of seeing the world and humankind's place within it. Fragments of these early literary traditions are echoed in the Hebrew Bible—for example, Mesopotamian and Egyptian flood legends are reworked in the story of Noah, an Egyptian tale called "The Two Brothers" finds an echo in the story of Joseph and Potiphar's wife, and the Hebrew Genesis finds inspiration in Mesopotamian and Egyptian creation myths.

The state religions of the ancient Near East and their rituals were closely tied to natural phenomena and focused on the maintenance of a properly functioning world. In Egypt, for example, the king was the only official celebrant of the ritual: In return for the proper offerings and actions, the gods gave him power and dominion over the land. However, for the bulk of the population, personal piety focused on gods of lesser national importance or on caring for the cults of deceased relatives.

The pantheons of the various cultures were for the most part large and complex and included many local gods and goddesses, who joined the national religious cults as their devotees were absorbed by the growing states. There was a great tolerance for these "foreign" deities, who were usually adopted rather than scorned. In general, ancient Near Eastern religion does not attempt to codify a single correct mythology or liturgy; in fact, three distinct creation myths coexisted peacefully during the historical period in Egypt.

A significant percentage of the wealth of the state was poured into the building of monumental temples, palaces, and fortifications. In Mesopotamia elaborate temples were set on top of terraced towers called ziggurats—ladders reaching into the sky. The Egyptian pyramid complexes, massive tombs surrounded by temples in which the royal funerary cult was celebrated, still stand as memorials to the centralized might and enormous wealth of these ancient kings. The recent discovery of the cemetery in which the men and women who built the Giza Pyramids were buried demonstrates their willingness to serve their rulers and underscores the effectiveness of these ancient political and religious systems. Both temples and palaces acted as centers for the accumulation and redistribution of surplus good and provided visible symbols of elite wealth and power.

CIVILIZATION APPEARED AND SPREAD at an astonishing rate during the period between the fourth and third millennia. With it came tremendous advances in art and technology, monumental architecture, the development of elaborate state-run religions, and the stratification of society. As trade networks expanded, the region became more tightly integrated. With the invention of writing came the historical period, and events in the lives of individuals, families, and nations could be reconstructed in greater detail.

As civilization became the dominant way of life throughout the Near East, powerful city-states and nation-states jockeyed for position in order to gain greater security and increase their access to raw materials and luxury goods from abroad. By the late third millennium the first empires arose in Mesopotamia, flexing their strength by exercising dominance beyond their natural or traditional borders. Over the course of the next three millennia, political and economic supremacy passed from state to state, ebbing and flowing as one empire fell and another rose from its ashes. Climatic changes—including the impact of humans on their environment—population movements, and individual personalities added their voices to the sounds of change that blew constantly over the mountains, valleys, and plains of the region.

A combination of inscriptional and archaeological evidence has allowed scholars to reconstruct the historical framework of the period from the middle of the second millennium to the middle of the first millennium B.C., although many details are still open to debate. The lives of the majority of people would not have changed much—more enlightened rulers might have made life easier or fairer for them, but their days would have continued to revolve around subsistence activities.

In about 2300, while the pyramid-building kings of the Old Kingdom held sway in Egypt, the Akkadians, a group belonging to the Semitic language family, built the first empire. They launched their armies from their northern Mesopotamian homeland into neighboring Sumeria under King Sargon I. In an early echo of the Moses story, Sargon was said to be the son of a nomadic father and a priestess mother, who set her infant adrift in a basket of rushes. He was found and raised by a peasant woman and eventually ended up as cupbearer of the king of the city-state of Kish. He led a revolt against his royal master, then took over the neighboring city-state of Akkad, and eventually built an empire.

A major period of drought and an unsustainable administration based almost entirely on military coercion led to the fall of the Akkadian Empire within 150 years; similar climatic conditions coupled with political weariness also caused Egypt to dissolve into a period of internal unrest and divided kingdoms. In about 2112 B.C. Urnammu of Ur created a new empire in southern Mesopotamia; he and his successors placed a great deal of emphasis on effective bureaucracies and formulated important codes of law.

In Egypt a new dynasty of rulers emerged from the southern town of Thebes, reunited the country, and built a stable and effective bureaucracy.

Like their Old Kingdom predecessors, the Middle Kingdom rulers of the next dynasty chose to move to the Memphite region, where the Nile Valley and Delta meet. From this vantage point they could control trade routes to the northeast; in addition, they built a series of fortresses to control their access to the riches of the lands to the south. These rulers planted the seeds of the later Egyptian Empire.

In the early second millennium, Semitic-speaking Babylonians had gained the upper hand in Mesopotamia and maintained control of the region for about 200 years. The last great king of the Babylonians was Hammurapi, who proclaimed himself "Strong King of Babel," "King of All the Land of Amor, Sumer, and Akkad," and "King of All Four Sides." He is famous for his code of law and for his effective and enlightened administration.

AT SOME POINT groups of people from the northeast, who spoke languages belonging to the Indo-European family, filtered into the region. During the 17th century B.C., as the Babylonian Empire was dissolving and the Indo-European Mitanni (also known as the Hurrians), based east of the Euphrates, were coming into their own, internal disputes and external forces coupled to fragment the control of the Middle Kingdom Egyptian rulers. These shifts in population throughout the Near East pushed many Semitic-speaking pastoralists and traders into the Nile Delta, where they founded a dynasty known as the Hyksos, from the Egyptian for "rulers of foreign lands." These intruders dominated the region for a century, acting as overlords to several vassal dynasties. They brought with them such technological innovations as the horse-drawn chariot, and they taught the native Egyptians the painful lesson that they were no longer safe within their own borders.

While the Hyksos were ruling in the Nile Delta, a powerful kingdom was developing far to the south, in the land of Kush. In the mid-16th century B.C. a line of rulers rose again at Thebes and began the process of driving out the Hyksos. The last of these, Ahmose, did not stop with routing the foreign invaders. He continued up the Mediterranean coast, and Egypt reentered the arena of international politics as a key player. The warrior-kings of the New Kingdom built an empire reaching from the Fourth Cataract in the south to the Euphrates in the north. The southern empire was under the complete control of the Egyptians, ruled by an Egyptian governor who had full access to the region's raw materials, especially gold. The northern empire was more of a sphere of influence, with vassal kings whose sons were raised in the Theban court, which ruled under the aegis of Egypt.

While Egypt was building its northern empire, it had to contend with the Mitanni and a new dynasty of Babylonians. After a series of bloody but ultimately indecisive battles, the superpowers resorted to diplomacy instead. Several New Kingdom rulers added Mitanni and Babylonian princesses to their harems, although they declined to return the favor and send Egyptian princesses abroad. A patchwork of city-states existed in the shadow of the superpowers, and vassal kings pleaded in vain with their Egyptian overlords for help against marauding tribes (often referred to as the Apiru and identified with the later Hebrews), and powerful allies reminded their Egyptian "brother" of promises of gold. At this time a new power, the Indo-European Hittites, defeated the Mitanni and upset the regional balance of power.

Hittite archives from their capital of Boghaz Keoy, in Anatolia, report that during the period just following the rule of Akhenaten, perhaps after the death of his successor, Tutankhamun, the Egyptian queen sent to their king, Suppiluliumas, begging for a Hittite prince to marry. After some hesitation a prince was dispatched, but he died en route to his royal wedding. From the same city, only about 50 years later, comes the record of a peace treaty between the Hittite king, Hattushili III, and his Egyptian counterpart, Ramses II (the Great); the same treaty is preserved on the walls of a series of temples built by Ramses himself.

The biblical Exodus has often been assigned to this period of Egyptian history, but, as yet, there is neither archaeological nor textual evidence from Egypt for the story as it is told in the Bible. The name "Israel" appeared for the first time during the reign of Ramses II's successor, Merneptah, on a triumphal stele, where it was identified as a nation of pastoralists occupying the highlands of the Canaan region.

The center of dispute among the skirmishing nations of the second millennium B.C. was the eastern coast of the Mediterranean, which held the key to control of the major trade routes. Maritime traders, such as the merchant-princes of the port city of Ugarit (Ras Shamra) and the sailors of the Aegean world, played a crucial role on the international stage. A shipwreck off the coast of southern Anatolia from about 1300 B.C. provides a snapshot of the times. The items on board included ten tons of copper ingots, raw material for bronze weapons; a ton of resin from Syria for use in Egyptian temple ritual; amber from the Baltic regions; elephant tusks, hippopotamus teeth, and ostrich eggs from the African southlands; and pottery for export from Canaan and the Aegean kingdom of Mycenae.

At the dawn of the tenth century, climatic change again led to waves of migration from the northwest. The Hittite Empire fell, and all over the Near East the power of the urban centers and their elite ruling classes declined. Many city-states along the eastern Mediterranean coast were destroyed by marauding groups of pirates who had themselves been pushed out of their homes. The Egyptians held on for a while in the face of attacks from groups of these raiders, known as the sea peoples, who included the Peleset (Philistines), but by the beginning of the first millennium B.C., Egypt's days of native glory had ended.

THE EARLY FIRST MILLENNIUM saw the rise of a new power, the Assyrians, whose homeland lay on the upper reaches of the Tigris River. These merchant-kings had been major players since Sumerian times because they controlled strategic desert and river trade routes. In the ninth century B.C. a series of despotic, bloodthirsty kings given to opulent displays of luxury and cruelty began to build an empire.

In response to the general upheavals and the aggression of the Assyrians, rural groups moved into the highlands, where agriculturalists and pastoralists formed loose federations. One of these federations formed the basis for the kingdom of Israel. The Israelites are thought to have been formed by two waves of migration from Mesopotamia to the hilly regions of Canaan, one in the 18th century B.C. and the other in the 14th century B.C. The patriarchal narratives of the Bible portray a semi-nomadic lifestyle based on the herding of domesticated animals. Sometime before the tenth century B.C. the Israelites gradually took over Transjordan, from present-day Anron in the south to Jabbok in the north. They were divided into tribes and governed by leaders known as judges.

After the tribes of Judah and Benjamin took over the Canaanite hill country near Jerusalem, they encountered the Philistines, former sea peoples who occupied most of the Syrian coast from Gaza to Joppa and had footholds in the heart of Canaan. Iron weapons gave the Philistines the edge, but they were finally defeated by David (1004–960 B.C.), who took over the cities of Canaan and united Israel as its first king. He controlled the trade routes through the area and conquered the city of Jerusalem, which he made into his capital. There he built a royal palace and a shrine for the principal god of the Israelites, Yahweh. He was succeeded by his son Solomon, during whose rule the Hebrew Kingdom reached its peak, rivaling Egypt and Assyria in power and prestige. The reign of Solomon, during which an extraordinary temple to the god of the Israelites is said by the Bible to have been built in Jerusalem, also saw conflict with external powers such as Egypt and Damascus, and internal dissent ended in a divided kingdom, with Judah in the south and Israel in the north.

During the next century, the kingdom of Israel made an alliance with the Semitic Aramaeans of Damascus in order to combat Assyrian aggression. But the Assyrian juggernaut was not to be stopped. In 722–721 B.C. King Sargon II conquered Israel and deported the Israelites. His son Sennacherib continued his conquests and even reached Egypt, where he was stopped by a pestilence that swept through his army. He was killed by a conspiracy, possibly engineered by his son Esarhaddon, who succeeded in conquering Memphis in only 15 days. But it was left to the next king, Assurbanipal, to consolidate the Assyrian conquest of Egypt, taking Thebes in 666 B.C.

Assurbanipal assembled a vast library at his palace in Nineveh, and its remains have provided modern scholars with an enormous amount of information about Mesopotamian culture and history. He was considered the greatest king of the Assyrian Empire, but his brother, Shamash-Shum-Ukin, who held Babylon, rebelled against him, and their civil war, which Assurbanipal won, presaged the downfall of the empire.

In 612 B.C. Nineveh was sacked by a coalition made up of Persians from Iran and native Babylonians. The Babylonians, under Nebuchadnezzar, ruled Mesopotamia for almost 50 years, but by 539 B.C., the armies of the Persian king, Cyrus the Great, had taken Babylon.

With the arrival of the Persians on the world stage, a new era of empire began. The Near East became in many ways a single unit, to be passed around by a succession of local and foreign armies. The various native cultures preserved many of their distinctive traits, but they became mixed with foreign influences to form a series of intricate mosaics. The path that humankind began to follow with the invention of agriculture had led, by the first millennium B.C., to a complex and interdependent world.

Colossal heads of Greco-Persian gods and a barely remembered king lie below a towering funeral mound at Nemrud Dagh, in Anatolia, south-central Turkey. King Antiochus I of Commagene considered himself a god in the first century B.C., before earthquakes and erosion despoiled his grandeur.

CHAPTER TWO

400 B.C. TO A.D. 1400

THROUGH
A GLASS DARKLY

ALEXANDER'S CONQUEST THROUGH THE CRUSADES

ANDREW WHEATCROFT

IN THE TOWN OF GORDIUM IN THE HEART OF ANATOLIA AN ancient legend held that whoever could unravel a knot binding a royal chariot to its yoke would rule the world. The intricate knot was covered with the hard, smooth bark of the cornel tree, so the rope was not visible and the task seemingly impossible. But in 334 B.C. the young Macedonian king, Alexander III, already a conquering hero, drew his sword and cut the knot in half. It was an act worthy of Hercules, the mythic half god/half man from whom Alexander claimed lineal descent. That night, according to Alexander's propagandists, thunder and lightning heralded the gods' approval of his deed. And over time the ancient prophecy seemed to bear out. Alexander's imagination imprinted the Middle East, and his legacy has endured for more than two millennia.

Alexander the Great was born in Macedonia, in what is now northern Greece, in 356 B.C. His father, Philip II, had turned the kingdom into the most powerful state in Greece. The key to their power was a revolution in military techniques: The Macedonian infantry phalanx—6,000 men in tightly packed ranks, one behind the other—were armed with pikes almost 20 feet in length. Normally, such huge bodies of fighting men were unwieldy, but Philip's troops could maneuver, changing pace or direction with polished ease. When the phalanx locked horns with the enemy, the Macedonian cavalry and skilled infantry-guards regiments moving with them would smash into the flanks of the opposing force. With this unique weapon, Alexander conquered most of the then known world.

In 336 B.C. King Philip was murdered by his bodyguard. The whole episode was shrouded in mystery. Some said Philip's assassination was carried out by a discarded former lover, others that it was the result of an obscure feud. But his death was extremely convenient for Alexander. At the age of 20 Alexander assumed power and two years later led his regiments through Thrace to the shores of the Hellespont—the Dardanelles—which separate Europe and Asia. A fleet of small boats carried his forces across the fast-flowing waters to the Asian shore. The sacred sites of Greece had been ravaged by Persian armies almost a century and a half before, and now, at last, a vengeful Alexander intended to repay their sacrilege with his own holy war. The Persian Empire that he aimed to conquer had declined a little from its former might, yet it was still the most powerful state between the Mediterranean in the west and the Himalaya in the east. Persian archers and Persian heavy cavalry were still incomparable, but there were few of them, and most who were then fighting for Persia's "Great King," Darius III, were Greek or Asian mercenaries.

About 40,000 Macedonians and Greeks crossed into Asia. With this powerful army Alexander fought his first battle with the Persians a few miles inland from the Sea of Marmara and emerged victorious. Soon, the Greek cities in Asia Minor had rallied to him. The history of his conquests is sometimes hazy, but with Alexander, myth and history merge into one. After his victory over the knot at Gordium, Alexander swung south, beating a Persian army at Issus on the shores of the Mediterranean. Then he moved on Egypt, and by 331 B.C. it had fallen to him. Doubling back, he thrust into the heart of the Persian Empire. The final battle with his old nemesis Darius came at Gaugamela, east of the Tigris and Euphrates in Mesopotamia. The huge Persian Army, drawn from every corner of their empire, was shattered by the control and discipline of the

Macedonians. In two years of campaigning Alexander had beaten Darius's best armies, then captured his capitals of Susa, Babylon, and Persepolis. Before Alexander could settle matters in a final battle, Darius paid the price of failure. He was murdered by his own officer, Bessus, who assumed the throne. Alexander's men found a muddy wagon containing Darius's blood-spattered corpse, still circled by the golden chains that symbolized a great king of Persia. So perished the last of the Achaemenid dynasty. Alexander wrapped the body in his own cloak and ordered a state funeral.

It had taken four years from the crossing of the Hellespont for Alexander to battle his way to Persepolis. He marched his armies farther east, reaching the Indus River, in modern Pakistan. Alexander wanted to keep going, but his men refused. The boundaries of his eastern empire were in essence those that Persian rulers established in the past, and he had proclaimed himself a great king, in the Persian style.

A king of Persia was the king of kings, a demigod who was dressed, Greeks averred, like a peacock, and who ruled a vast empire through a bureaucracy of officials and governors. His court practiced many customs that continued through the later Byzantine and Ottoman Empires, among them the seclusion of women and the employment of eunuchs. But its most visible characteristic was the use of luxury as a statement of power. The Greeks were horrified at this display of excess: A thousand animals were slaughtered each day for the great king's household, and a great dinner might have as many as 15,000 guests. But Alexander's empire extended beyond the old Persian sphere of dominance. He was also master of Greece and the Balkans. His domains yoked East and West together. He embraced both the Hellenic traditions of the city-state and the Persian customs of the great empire ruled through intermediaries and state officials. In doing so, he permanently altered the political and social structures of the region. Prior to Alexander, the Middle East as we now know it had been merely the western flank of the East, dominated successively by the civilizations of Mesopotamia, Egypt, and Persia. After Alexander, the lands between the Hellespont and the Nile were truly a midpoint, linked closely with both East and West.

In 323 B.C., at the age of 33, Alexander died of a sudden illness. He left behind a world of Greek cities and towns where before there had been few. This world, neither pure Hellenic nor pure Oriental, was a mixture of East and West. Alexander's Macedonian generals became "naturalized" to their new kingdoms. In Egypt Ptolemy I was crowned as pharaoh, while Seleucus became a hellenized version of a Persian great king. But what the Hellenistic lands lacked was the implacable dictatorship with which Alexander had held all his territories together. One later legend told how, at a marriage feast at the Persian city of Susa, Alexander had talked of all his peoples united in "one great loving cup." In his mind Greeks would marry local women, and over generations all his peoples would become one. This was the Greek vision of the whole inhabited world, the *oikoumene*, from which we derive the word "ecumenical." This idea of universality lay beneath the cultures of the Middle East, from the period of Roman domination throughout the centuries of the Byzantine Empire. The two great religions that thrived on conversion, Christianity and Islam, both developed here in a region whose politics had been shaped by the idea of boundlessness.

Between Alexander's death and the first intervention of the Roman Republic in the East, in 190 B.C., Greek-speaking rulers struggled for supremacy among themselves, just as the cities had fought each other in Greece before the rise to dominance of Macedon. But this endless political squabbling did not prevent the Hellenistic world from functioning as an economic unit. Many city-states on the Greek model lay between the borders of India and the Mediterranean. Goods were traded back and forth among them. Even areas outside this zone, such as the cities of Arabia, were intimately linked with the broader economy. Though Arabia stood outside the Greek-speaking political system, its aromatic gums, such as frankincense and myrrh, were in demand throughout the known world. Ports and cities grew up to service the trade within Arabia and as gathering points for the goods from India and beyond. The desert city of Palmyra and the port island of Bahrain had flourished on this trade for centuries. The economic links to the East from the Mediterranean had been well established before Alexander. With the growth of a Hellenistic empire, links between the Middle East and the West had expanded. Thereafter, under Rome's growing influence, the lines of connection increasingly ran west as much as east.

THE MIDDLE EAST IS, OF COURSE, A MODERN CONCEPT. Some now prefer its current synonym, Western Asia, or even the previous variant, the Near

East. "Near" in this phrase means close to Europe and is thus a product of Eurocentric ideas. "Western Asia" has redressed the balance, by making Asia the center and Europe the borderland. But "Middle East" at least reflects the fact that this region has always been pressured from both directions and in turn has pushed outward to both east and west.

If Alexander's conquests were deliberate, Rome's first involvement in the Middle East came grudgingly. To the Roman mind, the East always represented a social and ideological threat, as well as an economic opportunity. Rome's first eastward foray came during a war that lasted from 192 to 188 B.C. against the Seleucid rulers of Persia—descendants of Alexander's general Seleucus. By treaty Rome acquired territory south of the Black Sea. Some 50 years later, in 133 B.C., the king of Pergamum, Attalus III, bequeathed his kingdom—which stretched along the Mediterranean coast of Anatolia—to the senate and people of Rome.

For four generations Pergamum had been protected by the power of Rome, and Attalus had no obvious successor. He thought—rightly—that Roman rule was a better alternative for his kingdom than control by the predatory neighboring states. Christening this foothold the Province of Asia, Rome began a slow but inexorable expansion. In 63 B.C. Roman general Pompey added Syria, and with it a huge extension to Rome in the east, a veritable horn of plenty. But the resources and wealth of Egypt were even greater than those of the cities of Asia, and Rome coveted them. After Cleopatra VII (the last of the Macedonian Ptolemies) was defeated at the Battle of Actium in 31 B.C., Octavian, nephew of Julius Caesar, annexed Egypt.

From that point on, Rome was inextricably involved in the Middle East. Egyptian wheat fed the people of Rome. The taxes and treasures from the Middle Eastern provinces enabled Octavian, who renamed himself Augustus, the First Roman Emperor, to rebuild his capital on a grand scale. It was later said that Augustus had found Rome built of brick and left it made of marble. Although the East represented riches, it also held constant danger. Just beyond the eastern frontier lay the unconquered and unconquerable lands of Persia (or Parthia). And since the eastern and North African frontiers were desert, they offered none of the natural features, such as rivers, that Rome used in the West to establish a boundary or erect fortifications.

Despite these difficulties, at its height Rome's dominion extended from the Black Sea to the Red Sea and from the Nile to the Atlantic. Although the Hellenistic world had consisted of a scattering of cities, towns, and garrisons over a vast hinterland, Rome's control of its territories was well coordinated, systematic, and structured. Centered in towns and cities, its control also spread throughout the countryside. The prime difference between Hellenistic and Roman styles of government lay in Rome's sense of permanence. Roman rule was built to last. Nowhere was this more clearly visible than in the network of Roman roads, constructed to common standards, well maintained, and guarded. A traveler could, in theory, ride from the Gulf of Aqaba to the Atlantic coasts of France or Spain.

Still, the threat from the East was unremitting. War or the danger of war with Persia dominated Roman policy. There were major wars with Persia in the first three centuries A.D., and Rome's hold on the East weakened. In the third century Rome also lost control of Egypt, Syria, and most of Asia Minor to Zenobia, Queen of Palmyra. Soon thereafter, the Emperor Diocletian decided to divide the Roman Empire in two. It is some indication of the importance of the lands east of the Adriatic that Diocletian set up his own capital at Nicomedia in Asia Minor, leaving Rome and the west to his "junior" generals.

The Middle East seemed dangerous in more than purely military terms. It also threatened to undermine what Romans traditionally considered the guiding principles of their society. Imperial Rome had eventually settled upon the cult of the ruler, the divine emperor, as the official state religion. But this was a purely formulaic creed. As long as imperial subjects carried out the occasional ceremonies of emperor worship, they had the general liberty to revere whomever or whatever else they wished.

Many odd faiths, to Roman eyes, came out of the East—the popular bull cult of Mithras in Persia; the Egyptian cult of the goddess of fertility and motherhood, Isis; and in other parts of the Middle East, the worship of the mother goddess, Cybele, a transmutation of the Greek goddess Artemis. In Greece, she was depicted as a huntress, but in her great temple at Ephesus in Anatolia Artemis's statue had a torso bulging with multitudinous swelling breasts. The Hellenic huntress had become a potent Asian emblem of fertility, worshiped with orgiastic extravagance.

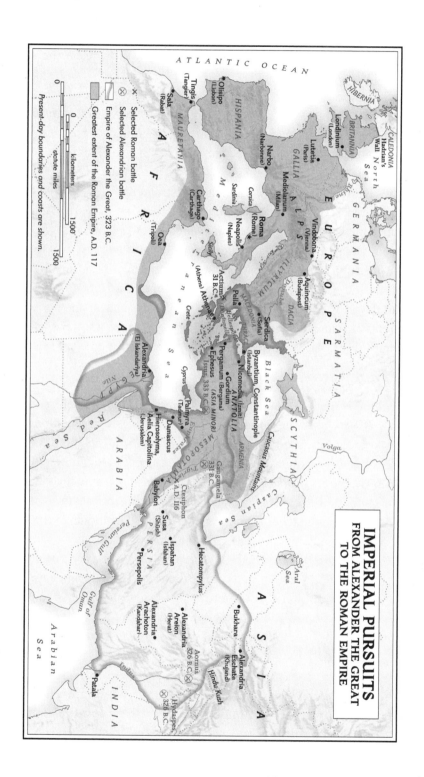

Other Asian cults reverenced Dionysus, the god of wine, in the same ecstatic fashion.

There were periodic halfhearted attempts to curb the sexual excesses associated with followers of Isis and Dionysus, while Mithras proved particularly popular within the Roman Army. But none of these posed any real challenge to the state. At the other extreme of belief and practice was the growing religious sect established by Jesus the Nazarene. The followers of Jesus, who had departed from their ancestral religion of Judaism, were incomprehensible and not a little repulsive to many Romans. To them, it seemed just another bizarre Oriental creed. They failed to recognize the uniquely powerful missionary effort by which Christianity was spread.

Christianity began as one of several reformist sects in Judaism, similar to the Essenes, who produced the Dead Sea Scrolls. Initially, it spread most rapidly through the network of synagogues, among Jewish adherents as a Jewish sect. But Christianity embraced non-Jews as well, opening the whole world to conversion. Stubbornly, many Christians refused to venerate any other gods and asserted that theirs was the only true faith. Weak and at first few in number, the Christians nevertheless worried the leaders of Rome. There were sporadic official persecutions. In A.D. 64 Nero used the Christians as a convenient scapegoat for a great fire in Rome. Many Romans agreed with the official position that the Christians were a contemptible, antisocial group, "hated for their vices."

Slowly, the religion that had begun as a Jewish sect started to acquire a significant number of believers in all classes of Greco-Roman society. A member of the imperial household became a Christian about A.D. 180 and began protecting fellow Christians in Rome from persecution.

By the end of the first century, there was already a well-organized Christian clergy, and regular news flowed among the believers along the excellent communications structure of the empire. The new faith became an international religion, from which the word "catholic"—meaning "spread throughout the whole" derived. As a pagan writer, Celsus, observed late in the second century, the Christians' strength derived from their cohesion. The Christian writer Tertullian insisted that "the blood of the martyrs is the seed of the Church." Tempered by persecution and organized around their bishops as spiritual fathers, Christians forged a structure and a collective discipline that amazed their adversaries. They also developed an extraordinary tendency to argue doctrine among themselves. Both tendencies—discipline and factionalism—were constant aspects of Christianity in the Middle East from the second century on.

In A.D. 260 the emperor Gallienus decided that the imperial government's preoccupation with the Christians was diverting it from its main task: resisting the growing pressure from enemies on the frontiers. From 261 to 303 all persecution ceased. Prominent Christian governors and military officials were now able to practice their faith openly. Property confiscated from Christians and their churches was restored. For some 40 years, Christianity spread even more rapidly than before. But in 303 persecution was renewed, when the emperor Diocletian was told that Christians had marred the state religious ceremonies by publicly making the sign of the cross with their fingers at a crucial moment. In 304 all the empire's citizens were ordered to make public sacrifices to the imperial cult on pain of death. Many Christians refused and were killed. Wide-ranging persecution of them spread, always more extensive in the East, where there were more Christians than in the West. Yet by 313 the wave of brutal public killings of Christians had clearly failed. They had not been cowed, and exemplary stories of their courage were quickly circulated among the Christian communities.

The shift in the state's attitude had been swift. After 304 imperial Rome devoted great efforts to destroying the growing power of Christianity. Even where there were no killings, Christian books, chalices, and church vestments were burned, while all church ceremonies were prohibited on pain of death. Diocletian retired to his palace on the Adriatic in 305, but the persecutions in the East were continued by his coregent, Galerius. Then, in 312, the new Emperor of the West, Constantine, reversed the tide. At the Milvian Bridge just outside Rome (parts of which still survive), he won a crucial battle against Galerius's son-in-law Maxentius, his rival for the imperial throne. Constantine attributed his victory to Christ's intervention, claiming he had seen a blazing cross in the sky. Halting the persecutions, he began to support the Christian cause, embracing it as a new and unified religion whose powerful God would support the empire. The alliance built between the emperor and the doctrinal power of the church was mutually advantageous. Most of the empire's citizens were still pagans, but gradually being a Christian became equated with being a good and dutiful Roman citizen.

In 325 Constantine called an ecumenical council of the church in the Anatolian city of Nicaea. Attended by about 220 bishops, it established an official creed for the Christian faith. In the same year Constantine began to build a new imperial capital, a "New Rome" that would be a Christian city in contrast to the pagan city of "old" Rome. He built it on the site of the ancient city of Byzantium on the European shore of the Bosporus. On May 11, 330, it was reinaugurated as the city of Constantine (Constantinople). Seven years later, shortly after he was baptized, Constantine died there, leaving a city that was still incomplete and ill equipped. Gradually, though, Constantinople became the preeminent city of the East, and the power of its archbishop grew accordingly, particularly after Emperor Theodosius I permanently moved the court there from Nicomedia.

By ABOUT 400 CHRISTIANITY WAS WELL ESTABLISHED as the official religion throughout the Roman Empire. It had spread first through Syria and Anatolia, then into Egypt and the cities of North Africa. But in the eyes of officials in Constantinople, the Middle East was also rife with heresy. The union between the power of the state and the authority of the faith required the state to enforce uniformity. If the emperors no longer claimed to be gods themselves, they held the uniquely powerful position of being the humble first servants of Christ. In the Christian East, there was a long struggle between orthodoxy, which ruled in Constantinople, and the heterodox sects that proliferated throughout the Middle East. Both traditions eventually coexisted, uneasily, side by side, with the Orthodox believers persecuting the sects whenever they had power enough to do so.

The essence of what we now call the Byzantine Empire possessed a theoretical unity, based on the union between church and state. But "heretics" continued to follow their own beliefs, and emperors as servants and representatives of the church occasionally persecuted them. In addition there was a growing division between Eastern and Western Christianity based on language. In the West, Latin had become predominant, especially in the church. In the East, it remained Greek, as it had been since the time of Alexander. By about 500 the church was clearly divided into language groups—Latin in the West, Greek in the East, and the languages of dissenting groups on the borders. When the Latin-speaking church evangelized, it insisted that the new converts adopt Latin, but the Greek-speaking church did not. It let the Slavs, as an example, develop a liturgy in their own language. The creation of this Christian liturgy in native languages would eventually help preserve those languages.

But language was not the only divergent element. Belief, too, was beginning to diverge, as dissident Christians in the East began establishing separate churches, with their own ethnic hierarchies—the Copts in Egypt, the Armenians on the eastern borders, and a number of sects in Syria and Palestine. It made these Eastern Christians unreliable allies for the emperor in Constantinople.

The powerful alliance between church and state caused a dramatic breach with the past. Previously in the Hellenistic world, diversity had predominated. Each city had its own god, each area developed slightly different structures of government, and that continued even within the Roman system. A town council in Egypt might seem superficially identical to one in Anatolia or Syria, but certainly they were not the same. The essence of the Byzantine system, on the other hand, saw uniformity as the highest goal. Constantinople strove to eradicate political anomalies, and the Christian bishops tried to root out heretics and dissidents. The state ensured that their leaders were deprived of office, their churches ransacked, and their books burned. Some dissidents escaped by moving out of the cities, or even across the frontier into Persia. The Orthodox hierarchy had some success, although religious uniformity was never quite as complete as its confident and triumphant claims suggested. Anomalies and what it considered heretical beliefs always revived.

With the accession of the emperor Justinian in 527, the attempt to construct a single, loyal, faithful Christian state became paramount. His near-ceaseless campaigns to recover the lands lost by the Roman Empire in earlier centuries and to extend the imperial frontiers were waged against many different enemies: the Persians, the Slavs in the Balkans, and the Vandal tribes in North Africa. Justinian created, in effect, a new society. Its northernmost frontier lay along the line of the Danube, then extended west to the Alps and Italy. Its southern flank lay in Egypt along the Valley of the Nile and along the North African shoreline. Inland, in eastern Syria, in modern Jordan, up the Nile, and along the long hinterland of North Africa, the desert and mountain tribes continued to control the land. There, Roman rule was little more than an illusion. Nonetheless, Justinian had dominion over a major part of today's Mediterranean Middle East, from the Black Sea to the northern tip of the Red Sea. Yet even there, where Roman rule had been restored, the desert flank from Arabia, through Syria to what is now Iraq, was open and left largely unguarded.

To Justinian and his successors, Persia posed the greatest threat. For a thousand years a succession of civilized cultures in Persia had challenged first the Greeks and later the Romans. Rome-in-the-West had already fallen to the "barbarian" tribes from the eastern steppes, but Rome-in the-East had succeeded in keeping the Persians at bay. It was not always easy. The new Sassanian dynasty had taken power in Persia from the Parthians in A.D. 224. Their first monarch, Ardashir, claimed descent from the ancient Achaemenids and, crowning himself king of kings, confronted the Romans. His son Shapur jettisoned the Hellenistic structures of the state, setting out to restore ancient Persian traditions. The worship of the god Mazda, through the teachings of his prophet Zoroaster, became the state religion, and Pahlavi rather than Greek became the language of the court and administration. The new Persia represented a coherent, powerful, and attractive alternative to Byzantine rule among many of the peoples along its western borders. Given the choice of the Persians or the oppressive Byzantine Greeks as overlords, many people preferred to throw in their lot with the Persians.

Early in the seventh century, the emperor Heraclius waged war against Persia. During the 18-year conflict, Heraclius lost control of Syria, much of Anatolia, and Jerusalem itself in the process. The challenges facing Heraclius were greater than any confronted by his predecessors.

But a more insidious pressure faced both Romans and Persians. A group of nomads set out from the regions to the east in Central Asia and moved west toward Europe and southwest into Persia. Called the Ruan-Ruan by the Chinese and the Avars by the West, they have faded from popular memory. Yet for centuries the Avars posed a constant threat. They were first subsidized by the Byzantines to attack other nomadic invaders, but their demands for payment rose precipitously. Unpaid, they ravaged the Byzantine lands in the Balkans and took their pay in booty.

Heraclius's greatest test came in 626, when Constantinople was besieged from the north by the Avar confederation and from the south by the armies of Persia. Faced by these great adversaries, he ignored the empty desert frontiers south and east of Anatolia. Traditionally, Byzantium's Christian Arab vassals, the Ghassanids, had patrolled these borders from their bases in former Byzantine fortresses ceded to them by Constantinople. Their chiefs were paid to keep the desert tribes (the Saracens) out of the empire. But controlling the incursions of desert raiders was very different from confronting the well-trained and well-equipped Sassanian horsemen and marauding Avars. The long war with Persia depleted the Ghassanids' military resources and also made the desert tribes less fearful of their retribution.

As Heraclius battled with Persia, distant Arabia remained in flux, and it was from the Arabian desert that the final, fateful challenge to Byzantine power in the Middle East emerged. Hardly the empty wasteland normally depicted, Arabia had thriving cities and ports, as well as a large reservoir of desert tribesmen who represented a wholly untapped military resource. What the Arab tribes lacked was coherence, organization, and discipline. Some had adopted Christianity or Judaism, but the majority still worshiped their personal, local, or communal gods. The individual who would ultimately transform the Arabs, and the known world, was an orphan named Muhammad bin Abdullah, born in A.D. 570 in the city of Mecca.

In his early adulthood, he managed camel trains trading with the city of Damascus. He had no learning or pretensions to sanctity. Yet, one night he became the channel for the word of God, uttered through his mouth. He recited what came to him. The Arabic for this poetic utterance is *quran*, and this was the name given to the words of God spoken through the mouth of the illiterate trader Muhammad. They were fine words, teaching one essential message. There was one God, announced by earlier prophets like Abraham, Moses, and Jesus. But the words God now spoke through this last prophet were his final and definitive statement. According to the Prophet Muhammad, only those who submitted completely to the power of God could understand his message.

The clarity and simplicity of these ideas would eventually appeal to many Arabs. But the people of Mecca, Muhammad's hometown, opposed him. In 622, when he was over 50 years of age, he led some 70 followers north to the city of Medina, to establish the new faith. That journey, *hegira* in Arabic, signified the birth of a new world for his followers, Muslims, who were the servants of God. As Christians divide history at the birth of Jesus, so Muslims began to record time at Year One of the Journey.

In Medina Muhammad and the Muslims created a new society, and they fought to defend it. The creed advanced by the Prophet recognized the realities of the world. It encompassed the organization of a state, the regulation of human life, and issues of war and peace. Those issues of political power, which Christianity developed slowly over time, were given directly by God to his Prophet. Unlike Christianity, Islam was never a hidden faith, growing strong in the shadows of the secular world.

From its early days, the Muslim community of believers *(umma* in Arabic) was strongly rooted in the concerns and problems of the world. The Prophet and his successors, the caliphs, imposed an iron discipline on the desert tribes. They fought to establish the principles of unity, as laid down in the blueprint given to the Prophet, who combined both the roles of religious leader and war chief. The Byzantine emperor was in some ways a similarly hybrid figure—in part a man of state, in part an arbiter of the faith. But he was never a prophet. In the persons of Muhammad and the leaders who succeeded him, government and faith blended indissolubly. The duty of the leader of Islam was to follow God's commandment, and God's imperative was to extend the umma throughout the world. This was the driving force behind Islam's rapid advance.

The Muslim leaders' zeal and capacity for war was first directed inward at Arab nonbelievers rather than at neighboring states. At first, these developments in Arabia seemed of little importance to either Byzantium or to Persia. They saw the Arabs as ill armed, shabby, disorganized barbarians. Both sides continued to battle one another, until, in 628, Heraclius finally emerged victorious. He had recovered both Jerusalem and the sacred relic of the Holy Cross, two events that seemed near miraculous. Heraclius had achieved as much in military terms as Justinian or Constantine. Yet in July 634 his triumph was overshadowed, when he heard news of a large body of desert raiders advancing from the south along the coastal plain of Palestine, either toward the port city of Jaffa or inland toward Jersualem. He dispatched a detachment south from Syria to disperse them.

Unbelievably, his well-equipped imperial troops were annihilated by these ragged warriors in a running battle south of modern Ramleh at a place called Ajnadain. The Muslims then beat a much larger Byzantine army on the Yarmuk River in modern Syria. Faced with these two wholly unexpected disasters, Heraclius recognized that the Muslims were no simple tribesmen on a raid and that, after losing two armies, he could not realistically hope to defeat them with the troops he had left. He immediately withdrew all his remaining forces north onto the high plateau of Anatolia. By the time he died in 641, the Byzantines effectively had abandoned control of Syria, Palestine, and Egypt to the Muslim invaders.

Thereafter, no one appeared able to stem the Arab advance. The desert warriors had defeated the Persians in 637, then had moved on Egypt two years later. By 642 their armies had pushed west, almost to the walls of Carthage in modern Tunisia. In 652 they had taken to the sea and their ships had raided Sicily. The Muslim armies built garrison towns such as Al-Fustat, south of modern Cairo, and Kufa, between Baghdad and Basra in modern Iraq. From these strongholds, they could both defend their new territories and keep their ideology pure and untainted. Daily prayers were strictly enforced, and the troops were given regular religious instruction.

The victorious Arabs initially lacked the stability provided by the solid political and administrative systems of Rome or Persia, and the first decades after the Prophet Muhammad's death were characterized by civil war and fratricidal strife. But the Arabs learned quickly. By the late 660s the first solid government, called the Umayyad Caliphate after a prominent Meccan family, took control of the Muslim world. Notionally, at least, the caliph, based in Damascus, commanded Muslims from the shores of the Atlantic in the west to what is now Afghanistan in the east. In practice, his authority depended on his military power. From the ninth century, actual power in the Middle East came to depend less on Arabs than on the Turkish slave soldiers called Mamluks, a word whose literal meaning is "owned" or "a possession."

The subsequent history of the Middle East was dominated by these interlopers, who came originally from the lands to the north and east of Persia. The Turkic nomads all spoke related languages but were divided into hundreds of clans and tribes. Turks made hardy, resourceful soldiers, and the Arabs soon used them to make up for the lack of manpower in the Arab armies. From the caliph's perspective, Turks captured in battle or bought as slaves were an especially valuable asset. They were entirely outside the tribal framework of the Arabs, with its complex of loyalties and enmities. Turks were foreigners, loyal to whomever owned them or paid them. As a result, Mamluks increasingly provided the bodyguards for the Arab elite and filled the ranks of the crack regiments.

IN 750 THE UMAYYAD CALIPHATE WAS OVERTHROWN and the entire Umayyad family pursued remorselessly. Only one survived, Abd ar-Rahman, who escaped to Al-Andalus (Spain) far to the west and joined those loyal to his family. There he set himself up as Emir of Córdoba in 756. The new Abbasid Caliphate failed to recover the west from the last of the Umayyads and instead focused on holding their domain in the east against many adversaries, including the resurgent Byzantines. They built Baghdad as their new capital, and thereafter the political importance of Damascus declined.

Factionalism proved to be the curse of the Islamic world, as it had been with Christendom. The unity of Islam was increasingly compromised by its fracture into numerous splinter groups. Traditional Sunni Muslims were the largest community, but there were many dissident (Shiite) parties. Although history can trace an endless succession of wars among Muslims, and Islam fragmented as rulers rose and fell, its basic political structures—whether used by Sunni or Shiite—nevertheless proved flexible and resilient. Islam quickly adapted the administrative culture of Persia and, to a degree, Constantinople to its needs. Later Muslim states were to reap the benefit of this resilient and efficient system of government.

Under the Abbasids, Islam developed into a creed that welcomed all comers. In the same way that Christianity had moved from being a Jewish sect to a world religion, so Islam gradually became less a faith for

Arabs than one with appeal to all peoples of the Middle East and beyond. During the fifth and sixth centuries, some Christians had found Zoroastrian Persia an easier master than Christian Constantinople. Likewise, many of the Eastern Christian sects in Syria and Palestine found Islam a less harsh overlord than the Byzantines had ever been. Many individual Christians in the East also found the clarity and simplicity of Islam attractive. They converted in considerable numbers. For those who did not, the theory of Islamic tolerance did not always match practice. The manner in which religious theory was translated into religious practice was closely related to political power. The more distant a region was from Abbasid power in Baghdad, the less authority the caliph could wield. Moreover, the power of Baghdad was waning. The last Abbasid ruler to exert real control came to the throne of Baghdad in 833, less than 25 years after Abbasid power achieved its zenith under the great caliph Harun al-Rashid. By the late ninth century, North Africa and Egypt had escaped from the Baghdad caliph's power, while in Muslim Spain the Umayyads' glittering capital at Córdoba rivaled any in the world. Increasingly, Muslim state fought against Muslim state.

In Egypt, Sunni and Shiite families vied for power. After 970 the North African Shiite Ismailis, or Fatimids (so called because of their descent from Fatima, the daughter of the Prophet Muhammad), took power. They set up their own Fatimid Caliphate in Cairo. Egypt became the alternative focus of power in the Middle East, and the united Muslim society fractured. Local Sunni rulers in Syria and Shiite Fatimids from Egypt all struggled to gain control of the region from the Anatolian plateau southward into Syria, Palestine, northern Iraq. Orthodox Christian Byzantines fought their own corner against all comers. But no one state was strong enough to achieve any more than a very temporary superiority, and this seemingly endless strife depleted the resources of all the adversaries. It is not surprising, therefore, that between 1000 and 1100 it was outside forces, first the Seljuk Turks from the East, then the Crusaders from the West, who exercised the decisive influence in a war-weary Middle East.

The period of Arab dominance in the Middle East was relatively short, at most 250 years. But in that time the entire region became comprehensively Arabized. Arabic became the language of state, the idiom of culture, and the voice of Islam. But for much of that time it was Turks, as slaves and later Muslim mercenary soldiers, who were the true power behind the throne. Outside the boundaries of the Abbasid Empire, the many clans of free Turks settled north of the Caspian Sea were growing in military power. In 1030 one group, called the Seljuks after their chieftain, moved into Persia and thence into Iraq. The Abbasids, locked in their endless struggle with the Fatimids, welcomed them as allies.

Between 1055 and 1060 the Turks took permanent control of Baghdad, claiming the title of sultan ("he who exercises power") and ruling on behalf of the Abbasid caliph. It was a convenient fiction. With the coming of the Turks, who were dedicated Sunnis, the balance of power shifted decisively against the Fatimids. In 1060 the Arabs yielded power to the Turks, but the newcomers adapted easily to the dominant Arab environment. In effect, the Seljuks only took openly the power that other Turks had exerted for decades.

The Seljuks swiftly took up the cause of Sunni Islam, first attacking Byzantine Anatolia, then overturning the Fatimid occupation of Syria, Jerusalem, and Palestine. In 1071 the Seljuks dealt a shattering blow to the Byzantines at the Battle of Manzikert (today's Malazgirt, close to modern Erzurum). The emperor Romanus was captured and his entire army killed or taken prisoner. The Byzantine Empire collapsed into civil war, and the Turks took over almost the entirety of Byzantine Anatolia in the space of seven years. In 1073 they moved south, conquering Jerusalem and Palestine. A vast new Muslim domain had been created, known as the Seljuk Sultanate, with its capital at Konya, in Anatolia. But their power continued to be opposed by many local Arab rulers and of course by the Fatimids, who had hitherto considered the Levant an integral part of their domain. The sectarian strife between Baghdad and Cairo had endured for more than a century, and although Muslims would shortly resist the invasion by the Christian West, it would be in an entirely piecemeal fashion.

As THE SELJUKS WERE ENTERING the Middle East, both the Christian West and the Byzantine domains were becoming increasingly preoccupied with Jerusalem. The millennium of the death of Jesus Christ fell in the year 1033-34, and Christians began to focus anew on his life and the land of his birth. At the time, Jerusalem was controlled by the fervent anti-Christian ruler of Egypt, al-Hakim. This Fatimid rule saw the Christian and Jewish presence in Jerusalem, also sacred to Muslims, as a defilement. All Muslims knew that the caliph Omar had decreed the building of the Noble Sanctuary (Haram al-Sharif) at the spot where the Prophet Muhammad had been taken on his Night Journey by the angel Gabriel. The Al-Aqsa ("The Farthest") Mosque had been built there, and it was an Islamic holy site as significant as Mecca and Medina. In his fanaticism, Al-Hakim had the Church of the Holy Sepulchre demolished, although the mountain of stones thus created was so vast that complete obliteration proved impossible. When he turned his cruel attentions to his fellow Muslims, he suddenly vanished from history. Al-Hakim's successors did not share his obsessions and allowed the work of rebuilding the damaged church to begin. But it was slow work and continued after the Turks took over the city in 1073.

Al-Hakim's phobic hatred of Christians and Jews was not shared by Muslims in general. Islam traditionally had made no effort to convert either Jews or Christians, and the Seljuks willingly accepted Christian pilgrims to Jerusalem. But the notion of the land of Christ's birth being desecrated and left desolate became increasingly powerful in the West. Thousands of pilgrims visited the Holy Land and brought back lurid tales of war, banditry, and the "alien" Muslim presence. Inexorably, the Christian West began to acquire a proprietarial feeling toward the "Holy Land."

In 1095 Pope Urban II, speaking to a huge crowd gathered outside the ancient Cathedral of Clermont in central France, called for Christians to recover Jerusalem. The impassioned response to his summons in France, Germany, the Low Countries, England, and Italy suggests that the idea of the Holy Land in danger was already present in people's minds. He had intended his call to be answered by kings, noblemen, and knights. In his mind, it was to be a pilgrimage in arms to recover the holy places. Urban referred to it as a pilgrimage, *peregrinatio,* but there was no doubt that he saw it as a military expedition organized and paid for by the monarchs, nobles, and clergy of Europe. Suddenly, though, it became a popular mass movement. Though the word "crusade" was never used by Urban, he did decree that all who set out should wear the badge of the cross—the emblem of Jesus Christ's death and Resurrection—on their clothes and banners.

Nothing like the First Crusade had ever been attempted before, or indeed subsequently. Those who took the cross displayed a mixture of blind faith, unthinking savagery, and extraordinary heroism under adversity. Each contingent leaving for the Holy Land followed a different trajectory. The popular crusade set out first, a rabble driven by faith. Some showed their hatred of those who denied Christ by robbing and then slaughtering the Jews of the Rhineland. Others pillaged and raped their way through eastern Europe all the way to Constantinople. But in Anatolia, almost 25,000 of them were killed by the Turks. The military crusaders took their time, arriving at Constantinople by sea and land. But of the 50,000 to 60,000 armed men who crossed over into Asia only about 7,000 were armed knights. They too lost many men and horses to the skillful Turkish archers on their rambling journey south. But they also made an impression on the Seljuks with their bellicosity, their blood lust, and their determination.

The crusaders marched through the heat of the summer in their chain mail. When their horses died, the knights rode on oxen. When the oxen died, they walked. The Westerners waged a kind of war that the Turks had never seen before. Finally, on June 7, 1099, more than two years after they had crossed into Asia, they arrived at their destination, Jerusalem. They scoured the arid landscape for wood and materials to build siege towers, knowing that a relief army from Egypt was on its way. Finally, the great mobile siege towers were ready, and early on July 14 their attack on the holy city began. By nightfall, Jerusalem was theirs. The crusaders were gripped by a blood lust so strong that the streets soon ran with the blood of the men, women, and children of the city. The Christians had won back the city for Christ.

The occupation of Jerusalem in 1099 created a crusader state called the Kingdom of Jerusalem. Geoffrey of Bouillon was elected as first ruler, but it was only after his death in 1100 that his brother Baldwin I took the title of king. This outpost of Western Christendom in the East lasted only until 1187. It was often called *Outremer*, old French for "beyond the sea." Later writers sometimes refer to it as a colonial possession. Perhaps so, but no Western state showed much interest in providing the money and men necessary to sustain it. Not much was left of the heady exuberance that had launched the First Crusade. The politics of crusading—who would lead the expedition and gain honor—became as important as any matter of faith.

Eventually, a Second Crusade set out in 1147 to succor Jerusalem, but it lost many of its men in battles and ambushes in Anatolia. It provided no worthwhile support for the beleaguered Westerners in the Holy Land. Thereafter, increasingly urgent appeals to Europe for help and support went largely unanswered.

In 1187 the ruler of Egypt, Saladin, shattered the crusader army at the Battle of Hattin and recaptured Jerusalem. A Third Crusade (1187-91), with the self-aggrandizing King Richard of England taking center stage, recovered some towns but failed to take Jerusalem. After 1192 only the remnants of the crusader state—a few castles such as Krak des Chevaliers (in modern Syria close to Homs) and such coastal towns as Acre and Antioch—remained in Western hands.

A Fourth Crusade was launched in 1202, but its sole success lay in storming (and looting) Christian Constantinople in April 1204. For three days the Westerners ravaged the capital of the East. One Western observer who was there said it was impossible to count the amount of gold and silver, plate and jewels, silks and furs that were pillaged. In his judgment, never since the beginning of the world had so much been taken in the capture of a city. The Venetians pillaged more systematically, taking home with them the four bronze horses that now grace St. Mark's Square. The Greek nobles and clergy fled the city. Western nobles, a new emperor, and Catholic bishops replaced them.

Constantinople-in-exile was established in small Byzantine successor states on the Black Sea and in Anatolia. In 1261, from one of these—the "empire" of Nicaea—an energetic Byzantine general named Michael Palaeologus saw the opportunity to push the by then decrepit Latin emperor and his few troops from the throne. But it was impossible to recover the strength and unity of the old Byzantine state, which continued the slow decline that the Western occupation had only exacerbated.

In the waning decades of the crusading movement, only one venture achieved any significant result. The Sixth Crusade, led by Emperor Frederick II in 1228, reacquired Jerusalem by diplomatic negotiations, but only for ten years. It then reverted to Muslim rule. In 1248 a new attack, led by King Louis IX of France, was launched on Egypt, as a first step to the Holy Land. It failed in front of the walls of Cairo, where the French king was captured. The final vestiges of the crusader state were removed when the rulers of Egypt campaigned through Palestine and north along the Mediterranean coast to expel the remaining Westerners. In 1271 the great castle of Krak near Tripoli was captured. With the fall of the port of Acre (in the modern state of Israel) in 1291, the Latin presence in the Middle East was virtually finished. Only the island of Cyprus remained in Western hands as a pale shadow of the crusaders' former glory. The Egyptian rulers devastated the land all along the coast so that the crusaders might never be tempted to return. Fifty years afterward, the traveler Jacob of Verona visited these ruined cities and found their shattered buildings eerily vacant, apart from a few Bedouin.

The crusader state left few physical vestiges of itself in the Middle East, save for a few vast castles and some other great buildings. But it created a new and lasting antipathy to the West in Muslim minds. Before the coming of the crusaders in 1097-99, few Muslims had any notion of the West. At best, they knew Westerners only by repute, as pallid and dirty creatures living in atrocious climates far to the north. But in response to the Christian holy wars, the Muslim idea of a war for the faith (jihad al-asghar), which had been largely ignored since the first century of Islam, revived and grew stronger.

In the last years of the crusader presence in the Middle East the region faced a new and deadly challenge. The Mongol horde had emerged from north of China and pushed out through the heart of Asia, whence the Seljuks themselves had come almost two centuries before. Turning west, the Mongols ravaged eastern Europe between 1237 and 1241. Then they moved on the Middle East. The Seljuks, whose empire had been established with the victory at Manzikert in 1071 and had survived the crusader onslaught, were no match for the Mongols. After the Seljuk defeat in battle at Kosedagh, in Anatolia, the Mongols immediately fanned out to occupy most of the the former Seljuk domain.

The few crusaders remaining in the East saw this invasion as an act of God, the weapon sent to defeat the infidel Muslims. At first, this divine intervention seemed likely to overturn generations of Christian defeat. They rejoiced when in 1258 the Mongols, led by Hülegü, besieged Baghdad, still a symbolic and cultural center of Islam. The Mongols slaughtered the population, including the last of the Abbasid caliphs, when they resisted demands to surrender. Hülegü's horde then moved northwest, attacking Syria, then occupying Palestine and Jerusalem. But the succession to the Mongol throne was in dispute, and much of the horde returned to the East. The ruler of Egypt, seeing his opportunity, counterattacked the denuded Mongol armies. In 1260, at the Battle of Ain Jalut, near Nazareth, the invincible Mongols were defeated by an army led by Sultan Baybars.

Baybars was one of the River (Bahri) Mamluk, so called because the barracks of these particular Turkic slave soldiers was on Rhoda Island in the middle of the Nile. Their leaders ruled in Egypt from 1250 to 1382. And after their victory over the Mongols, Egypt became the preeminent Turkic state in the Middle East. The Mamluk dynasty in Egypt dominated from the Nile to the Anatolian plateau. But up on the plateau, another much smaller state was coming into being, one that would eventually end Mamluk power.

The tribe of Osman ruled the small Anatolian fortress town of Söğüt, equidistant between Ankara and the Mediterranean coast, on the frontier of the Byzantine lands. Known now as the Ottoman Turks, they gradually extended their small foothold toward the Sea of Marmara to the north. In 1333 Osman's son Orhan seized the town of Bursa, one of the few remaining outposts of the depleted Byzantine Empire in Anatolia. The Ottomans quickly extended their territory north to the coast until they occupied all the land south of the Hellespont, where Alexander the Great had landed centuries before. But they were only one of many Turkish principalities in Anatolia, with a Mongol state to the east. The future for the Ottomans lay not in Asia but across the narrow waterway in Europe.

Though the Byzantines had lost their last few places of strength in Anatolia, they still held large territories on the European shore. But the complex rivalries in Constantinople had led to constant challenges to the emperor's power. Unwisely, in 1345 Byzantine emperor John VI Cantacuzenus invited the Ottomans to send troops to help him against his own son-in-law. The Ottoman armies, led by the sultan's son, Süleyman, crossed the Hellespont into Europe, thus reversing Alexander's journey of conquest. Less than a month after their arrival, a powerful earthquake shook the European shore. Some presciently said it was a dangerous omen of what the coming of the Turks would mean.

ALMOST 17 CENTURIES SEPARATED these two short journeys: Alexander going south to conquer, Süleyman going north. Alexander, or Iskandar, was as much a legendary hero to Muslims as to Christians. In many respects, Muslim rulers embodied the larger part of Alexander's vision. Like him, they saw no limits or boundaries to their conquest. In the culture of Islam, as in the Macedonian oikoumene, there was no sharing of power. Although Alexander was happy to become a great king in the Persian style, admiring and enjoying the luxuries of the East, he knew that Hellenistic culture surpassed all others. Everyone in his empire was invited to unite and drink from the "great loving cup," but power in the Hellenistic world was to be held by the Macedonians and the Greeks. Likewise, in the Middle Eastern Muslim society, indigenous Christians and Jews were usually free to practice their faith, but they were inferior and without power. Only a Muslim, by birth or conversion, had any significance in this world.

In the empires that ruled in the Middle East—Persia, Alexander's and those of his Hellenistic successors, republican Rome, imperial Rome, the Byzantine Empire, and Islam—change and continuity existed side by side. Historians often tend to emphasize radical changes and stark transitions, but this makes little sense in the context of the Middle East. The connections and continuities from antiquity into the modern era often have been obscured by modern scholars, and, as a result, in the words of the Christians' St. Paul, perceived "through a glass, darkly."

During the long centuries between Alexander's entry into the Middle East and the rise to power of the Ottoman Turks, momentous changes occurred, among them the rise and fall of the Roman Empire and the births of Christianity and Islam, religions that would come to encompass the world. But these changes rarely obliterated what had gone before. Christians and Jews, who had spread throughout the East as a consequence of Rome's empire, continued to live in their communities under Muslim rule, preserving a continuity with their own past. They were not transformed or altered in any profound sense.

Nowhere was the constant presence of this distant past more evident than in Egypt. There, from the minarets of the new city of Cairo built by the Muslims, the pyramids were visible on the skyline. The Sphinx and all the physical evidence of Egyptian antiquity were reminders of a world before Rome, before Christ, and before the Prophet Muhammad. A world where the past and present melded into one another and forever colored the future.

"A triumph of harmony, proportion and elegance," the 17th-century Blue Mosque was built by Sultan Ahmet I to outshine the beauty of the great shrine to Christendom, Hagia Sophia (background). Together, these towers of faith dominate the skyline of Istanbul—or, as it was known for a thousand years, Constantinople.

CHAPTER THREE

THE OTTOMAN AGE

ANDREW WHEATCROFT

THE EMPEROR JUSTINIAN, THE SECOND FOUNDER OF THE
Roman Empire, built what has been described as "the last great architectural monument of the ancient world." His Church of the Holy
Wisdom, Hagia Sophia, dedicated on Christmas Day 537, was the
third built on the tip of the promontory overlooking the Bosporus, the
finest site in Constantinople. Justinian was determined to outstrip all
the earlier churches. He put 10,000 men to work on the new building
and ordered that virtually the whole of the interior be covered in
mosaic, while the sanctuary alone contained almost 40,000 pounds of
silver. But on May 29, 1453, this emblem of Christianity in the East,
the cynosure of the "True Faith", ceased to be a Christian church. On
that day it became the chief mosque of a newly Islamized city and was
stripped of its treasures.

The armies of the Ottoman Turks, led by the young sultan, Mehmed
II, known thereafter as The Conqueror *(Fatih)*, had finally taken the symbol of Christendom in the Middle East. Mehmed had no desire to

destroy what had long been the prophesied goal of the Islamic conquests. The first Muslim army to reach here only managed to camp outside the city in 670, defeated by the massive triple walls built by the Emperor Theodosius II. But in 1453, the Turks made huge cannon that slowly battered gaps in the ancient defenses. Mehmed's ambition was to become a Roman emperor and possession of the city gave him the title.

The West had done little to sustain Constantinople, yet loudly bewailed its loss. There were calls for a new crusade. Proclamations for this venture were some of the first texts to be printed on Johannes Gutenberg's recently invented press, and after them followed thousands of books and pamphlets dealing with the new problem of the Ottomans. These Turks had first appeared from the east from the steppes north of Persia in the mid-13th century, according to legend an insignificant band of some 400 nomad warriors. Unlike some nomads, they were fervent Muslims. The Seljuk sultan gave them a small town called Söğüt on the Anatolian border of the Byzantium and close to the modern city of Eskisehir. There they lived by raiding and plunder, while claiming a religious motivation for their way of life. In reality, like interlopers everywhere, their main purpose in raiding was economic, a means to survival in a harsh land. In 1326 these Sons of Osman, Osmanlis, after the name of their clan leader, took the substantial city of Bursa, on the slopes of Mount Uludag (the famous Mount Olympus of Mysia). From that point onward the Osmanlis—or Ottomans, as the West later knew them—were a major power in western Anatolia.

In 1345, 19 years after they captured Bursa, the Ottomans crossed the narrow waters of the Hellespont into Europe. They came as mercenaries in the service of the Byzantine emperor, John VI Cantacuzenus, but they soon overwhelmed their employer. Conquest in Europe was a much better prospect than squabbling with other Turkish princelings for Anatolia. In 1362 they seized the old Byzantine city of Adrianapole, less than 150 miles west of Constantinople, and made it their new, European capital. Moving north, in 1371 and 1389, they demolished the army of the most powerful Slav state in the Balkans. The battle in 1389, at the Field of the Blackbirds on the plain of Kosovo, became a symbol of Serb humiliation and of unstoppable Ottoman advance. By the early 15th century the Ottomans were much more powerful in Europe than they were in their Anatolian homeland. The contrast is very evident from the career of Sultan Bayezid I, whose nickname The Thunderbolt gives some indication of his skill in war. In 1396 he annihilated a Western crusader army at Nicopolis on the Danube. But only six years later he himself was comprehensively beaten at the Battle of Ankara and taken prisoner by the army of Timur, a new conqueror from the East who was half Turk, half Mongol.

From that point on, the Ottomans' strength in their northern, European dominions sustained their threatened domain in Anatolia. The limit of their ambitions lay on the Anatolian plateau and perhaps farther east into Persia. Militarily, perhaps, the Ottomans could have taken Constantinople 40 or 50 years before it actually fell into their hands. But by 1400 their nomad state had exceeded its organizational limits and political capacity. During the first half of the 15th century a slow transformation took place. They began to build the basic elements of a state structure that would lift the Ottomans above all the previous Turkish nomad states, most of which had disintegrated into warring factions that allowed some new conqueror to overcome them.

The Ottomans traditionally suffered from many of the same structural problems. Ottoman sultans fought with other powerful leaders in their clan and, frequently, with members of their immediate families. But slowly, to some degree because they were rooted part in Europe and part in their clan lands in Asia, they began to build a hybrid system. They adapted elements from their tribal past, from the Persian and Byzantine systems of government, and from their experience in ruling Europe. The Ottomans seemed to possess the luck and the instinct to make the right pragmatic judgments. The matter of slave soldiers was one strong example. Every Eastern state, since the time of the Umayyad caliphate, had employed Turkish slave soldiers (and later, Turkish mercenaries). So did the Ottomans, but in gradual stages they refined and transformed the slave system. Now that the Turks were Muslim, they could no longer (officially) be enslaved, so the Ottomans had to look elsewhere for their manpower. They admired the resilience of the Balkan Slavs and acquired many of their slaves from the Christian communities of Europe. But instead of waiting to enslave only captives from wars, they began to institutionalize the gathering of state slaves. Every three years or so, Ottoman detachments would set out to select a set number of "recruits" from the Christian communities.

This was different from the slavery of the American South in later centuries. Ottoman sultans came to regard their slaves as the most valuable asset of their state. These young men, mostly Christian by origin, were brought to Constantinople and expected to convert to Islam. Most became the highly trained infantry soldiers, called the new troops or janissaries, who provided the Ottoman rulers with a unique advantage over all other states. A chosen few slaves were trained as civil servants. Soldiers or bureaucrats, these state slaves were free from the local or community ties that circumscribed the Turkish clans. State slaves owed loyalty only to the House of Osman. These janissaries and administrators were paid, clothed, and housed by the sultan, and those who showed promise progressed rapidly to high positions in the military or state service. Even grand viziers, the most senior officials of the state, were often drawn from this slave recruitment. The Ottoman sultans were also extremely astute in how they used their human resources. They would deploy their European soldiers against enemies in their eastern lands and would then send Anatolian levies to fight in Europe. No person of high rank was ever posted to serve in an area where he had tribal or family connections.

Over time the word "Ottoman," which had originally meant the Turkish clan descended from Osman, eventually included not only the sultan and his family but the whole ruling elite of the empire. Ottoman became a cultural term, meaning a member of the cultivated and educated ruling class. An Ottoman eventually meant someone of refined tastes, who could read and write elegant Ottoman Turkish, a poetic language full of high-flown Arabic and Persian phrases. The ethnic word "Turk" on the other hand, became an insult, meaning a crude peasant. This Ottoman ruling class was not Turkish but was drawn from almost every nation within the empire. For the most part its members were united by their common Muslim faith, although in later centuries even Christians and Jews had their place within the system, as Ottomans. The Greek Orthodox patriarch in Constantinople was Christian, but he also had the official status of a pasha—after a vizier, the highest rank of the civil and military hierarchy.

LIKE THE ROMAN EMPIRE, the Ottoman Empire found a means to bind its elites together within a common Ottoman identity. Its critics said, with some justice, that the Ottoman ruling class became equally contemptuous of all its subjects, whatever their nation or faith. In Ottoman eyes their empire contained only two fundamental categories. One was the Ottomans themselves, the ruling class, and the other was all those over whom they ruled. In a phrase redolent of their nomadic, herding origins, these underlings were called the flocks, for which the Turks used the word *raya*—"those who paid taxes." These anonymous human beings were to be used for the benefit of the rulers. It made little difference whether they were Muslim or belonged to other faiths. All, in varying measure, were exploited for the benefit of the ruling group. Among the raya, each community was defined not by race or color but by religion. The Christians and the Jews were largely self-governing within their communities, under the control of their own religious leaders, who were responsible for their good behavior. Muslims too were often administered by their own local leaders, who had been incorporated within the Ottoman structure. So long as the flocks were quiescent and paid their taxes, the Ottoman yoke was generally relatively light. Only if the communities failed to submit—or more frightening still for the rulers, rebelled—did the full, brutal weight of Ottoman power fall upon them.

In the 60 years after the capture of Constantinople in 1453, the Ottoman capital acquired many new names. Constantinople was arabicized as Konstantiniyye. It was often called the Abode of Bliss. The most fanciful was Islambol, a made-up word meaning "the city of Islam." Istanbul or Stamboul lasted longest. Its origins were also unclear, but it was probably a Turkish version of the Greek phrase *istinpolin*, meaning "in the city."

In those decades, the Middle East below the Anatolian plateau saw little of the Ottomans. Nothing much had changed in the flourishing port cities along the eastern Mediterranean shore for many generations. The Mamluk rulers of the region were far away in Egypt. Many of the Arab families, the notables, who formed the elite in cities on the coast and inland had been there for generations. In 1514 the new Ottoman sultan Selim—nicknamed The Intrepid because of his boldness in war (and perhaps because he had forced his father to abdicate and had killed all his brothers)—turned a border war with the Persians in the east and the Mamluks to the south into a full-scale campaign. At the Battle of Chaldiran in 1514, Selim's janissaries and field artillery defeated a larger army of Persian horsemen. The Persian capital of Tabriz taken, Selim turned southwest to meet Persia's Mamluk allies. Once again Ottoman discipline triumphed and Selim advanced through Syria toward Egypt. He pushed aside one Mamluk army close to Gaza, beat another inside Egypt in January 1517, and took Cairo.

The Mamluk leaders were systematically put to death, and Selim returned to Istanbul with Syria, Palestine, and Egypt, as well as Mecca and the western coast of the Arabian Peninsula, under his control. He brought back with him some sacred relics of the Prophet Mohammed, as well as the title of caliph, which the last surviving Abbasid then living in Egypt had relinquished to him. For the people of the Middle East, one overlord taking the place of another had little immediate consequence. It was the Ottomans who were transformed by taking control of the Arab lands. Trade between the Middle East and the states of Western Europe now came under Ottoman rule, and the Ottoman Peace (*Pax Ottomanica*) created a free market between all the lands under their control. Trade grew not only between the West and East (mostly carried in the ships of French, English, and Dutch merchants) but within the new empire itself. There was a flourishing market in Istanbul, Cairo, and many of the smaller cities of the empire for goods produced in other Ottoman-ruled regions.

Selim took radical steps to keep his enlarged empire united. With a cruel but ruthless pragmatism, he killed off all his sons but the eldest, Süleyman, to avoid the contested succession that had divided the ruling family in the past. Under later sultans younger brothers were not killed but kept in a secure (if gilded) imprisonment. This was not from greater tenderheartedness but from a fear that, with the high infant mortality, too radical a cull would leave no heirs to the throne.

Süleyman I became the archetypal Ottoman. He waged war with zest, and considerable success. He had a splendid court, which led to Westerners naming him The Magnificent. His own subjects called him The Lawgiver (*Kanuni*), and he instituted a vast structure of imperial law that went far beyond the Islamic *sharia* code, the greatest codification since the days of Justinian. His wars were likewise on a truly epic scale. Many thousands of his soldiers and a vast fleet captured the Aegean island of Rhodes in 1522, and he himself destroyed the Hungarian Army at the Battle of Mohács in 1526. Three years later he besieged Vienna from late September to late October. But waging war so far to the west, the Ottomans were operating at the limits of their range. They sought to avoid fighting over the winter season. Once it was clear Vienna would not fall, and the weather got colder, they retreated. In 1566 Süleyman tried again, wisely starting earlier in the year. His advance was held up by a small but stubbornly defended fortress of Szigetvár, and the old sultan died in early September before his armies reached the Austrian capital. It was more than a century before Ottoman armies again laid siege to Vienna.

For most of his long reign Süleyman concentrated his energies not on war in Europe but in the Middle East and the Mediterranean. He fought a long series of campaigns against Iran, securing Ottoman possession of modern Iraq and consolidating Ottoman power in the Red Sea: he extended his father's conquests in Arabia as far as Yemen and the shores of the Indian Ocean. Although Süleyman was himself a warrior on land, much of the Ottoman expansion took place through the long reach of the empire's naval power.

The North African coast between Egypt and Morocco became the main battleground. Port cities such as Algiers had built large fleets of war galleys, which raided enemy shipping in the Mediterranean and ravaged the coasts of Spain and Italy. Süleyman shrewdly appointed the ruler of Algiers, known as Barbarossa, as admiral of the entire Turkish fleet, and their combined strength dominated the sea-lanes. The corsairs from Algiers, Tunis, and Tripoli became in effect state-protected pirates, enriching themselves, their home ports, and the Ottoman treasury. Holy Roman Emperor Charles V, the Habsburg ruler of Spain, with ambitions to build an empire in North Africa, reciprocated by attacking the corsair ports. The attacks on Tunis and Algiers were depicted in the West as a new crusade, with the vague hope that Jerusalem might ultimately be recovered for Christendom. This naval warfare became the main Ottoman battlefront, and gradually the North African cities were incorporated into their domain.

But Süleyman's reputation was built on more than war. His legislation created the model to which all later Ottomans aspired. Throughout the Middle East Süleyman ensured that the existing elites were progressively co-opted into the Ottoman system. The slave recruits of earlier generations were increasingly replaced by freeborn Muslims, who were attracted by a profitable and honorable career in the Ottoman bureaucracy or the Ottoman war machine. There was a constant movement not just of goods but of people. Families from Istanbul would move to Aleppo or Jaffa to make their fortune. Albanian or Serbian Muslims from Europe made their career in Ottoman service and could easily end up in Egypt, Syria, or Yemen.

From the late 16th century on, Westerners began to give excessive credence to tales of Ottoman decline. They could not perceive the hidden resilience in the system created by Mehmed the Conqueror, Selim the Intrepid, and Süleyman the Lawgiver. Europeans fantasized lubriciously about life in the harem. They shuddered at the undoubted harshness and cruelties of the Ottoman system, and endlessly retold tittle-tattle about debauched or mad sultans and the pashas' venality. Yet even in these negative accounts, unintentional hints of a powerful, if sometimes wayward, government kept coming to the surface. Presenting the minutiae of Ottoman rule was much less exciting than stories of odalisques and bizarre passions, but they were the mundane reality. The Ottoman Empire was all about bureaucratic legalities and paperwork. The European states would also develop along the same lines. While there was undoubtedly a decline, it is very hard to pinpoint precisely when it began. Time and again, these supposedly torpid failing Ottomans would inexplicably rouse themselves, raising an army or a fleet, and would strike back decisively at Western encroachment.

There was a time of transition, and it came early in the 18th century. While the balance sheet of territorial gains and losses remained roughly equal, the failure of the Ottoman attempt in 1683 to capture Vienna, and the subsequent loss of land in Hungary and the Balkans, was a turning point, at least in the west of their empire. But while the Ottomans began to weaken in the west, they faced no equivalent challenge in the Middle East. Yet difficulties in the west certainly had repercussions farther east. On the desert frontiers, Ottoman power historically had extended only to the point where Ottoman troops could enforce the sultan's decrees. Increasingly, demands for troops and money to sustain resistance on the European frontier drained Ottoman resources in the Middle East. Moreover, the janissaries who had settled in cities like Damascus or Aleppo declined to be recalled to military service. They still drew their pay, but they had no interest in going to war in the desert or far away in Europe.

In the aftermath of the defeats beginning in 1683, Ottomans began to question whether they might have something to learn from the West after all. Many of the military problems on their 3,000-mile border were similar to those that had confounded the Romans almost a millennium and a half before. But while Rome had faced a great power (Persia) in the east, the Ottomans confronted challenges from powerful states in both east and west. The Habsburgs attacked them through the Balkans, Russia along the Black Sea, and Venice in the Adriatic. Between 1733 and 1736 the dynamic ruler of Persia, Nadir Shah, also occupied much of modern Iraq and pushed deep into Anatolia. Yet still the Ottomans survived, losing territory on the northern frontiers but ultimately defeating the Persians and remaining unchallenged in the Middle East. But they could no longer rely on the janissary system that had served them so well in the past. They needed an army and navy that could use the technology of Europe.

In the 18th century Westerners increasingly portrayed the Ottomans as ignorant, indolent, and pursuing pleasure to any possible excess. They were thought completely decadent, a mere shadow of their former strength and glory. Much the same had been claimed of the Roman Empire. Between 1776 and 1788 Edward Gibbon wrote a series of majestic volumes titled *The Decline and Fall of the Roman Empire*. The project took most of his adult life. He decided on this grand topic, he confided in his memoirs, on October 15, 1764 while sitting "amidst the ruins of the Capitol" in Rome. Gibbon was unsure whether to write in French or English, but his book would have been one of the world's greatest histories in either language. The last volume of *Decline and Fall* dealt with the rise of the Ottomans. Gibbon assumed that like the Romans before them their empire would also "fall." It lasted far longer than the West ever expected. In part Ottoman survival was helped by good fortune and the disunity of its enemies. But there was an inner defensive strength that enabled it to weather even greater storms in the 19th century. In the very last days of the empire, during World War I, the Western powers discovered that their long-despised Turkish enemy could still inflict defeats upon them.

What were the secrets of Ottoman endurance? In the first place, the system did not ultimately depend on individuals. It would certainly thrive under a powerful and active ruler, but it did not crumble in the weak hands of incompetent sultans. For 14 generations, from the mid-13th to the late 17th century, son had succeeded father at the head of the House of Osman. No European state at that time could claim that degree of longevity or relative stability. Then, after 1453, as the empire extended and then consolidated, its bureaucrats continued to collect taxes and customs tariffs and administer the laws regardless of who ruled in Constantinople.

Ultimately, all political structures fail, and from the late 17th century on, the institutions created by Mehmed II and his descendants began to decay. During the 18th century some sultans and their advisers recognized the need to modernize. Their vision of change was initially limited and very practical. The arts of war were what they wanted—not the culture of the West. But gradually they came to realize that administrative, economic, and educational reforms were the foundations of a successful state.

THE OTTOMANS HAD ALWAYS BEEN PRAGMATIC innovators, from the point in 1453 when Mehmed II had the inspiration to create huge cannon to batter the walls of Constantinople. Their palace of Topkapi was full of paintings, clocks, books, and the other productions of the West. But innovating sultans faced a vast body of conservative opinion deeply resistant to change. In part this was centered in the religious authorities called the ulama, who were fearful that change would undermine Islam. But others, like the janissaries, knew that modernization could undermine their powerful and protected status. Even the estimated 80,000 scribes in Constantinople, who wrote the books used in the empire, resisted the introduction of the printing press. Faced with these enemies, progress could only advance slowly and cautiously. One sultan, Selim III, who tried to modernize, was strangled for his pains in 1808. His ultimate successor, Mahmud II, eventually changed the centuries-old pattern of the empire. But even he had to proceed with great caution lest he suffer the same fate as Selim III.

Mahmud II inherited an empire that had already been severely undermined in the Middle East. A new Mamluk dynasty had recovered control of Egypt in the 1750s, occupied the Ottoman-ruled lands in western Arabia, and then invaded Syria. Egypt was recovered by an Ottoman army in 1785, but in 1798 Napoleon sailed with a French army into the East, invading Egypt, then marching north up the Mediterranean coast. Ottoman resistance to the French was led by a young officer, born in what is now Albania, called Muhammad 'Ali. After the French were driven out by a British expeditionary force, he took control of Egypt. Thereafter, until his death in 1849, Muhammad 'Ali autocratically transformed Egypt into the kind of powerful modern state that his overlord in Constantinople wanted for the whole of his empire. Egypt provided an exemplar for Mahmud. In Cairo in 1811, Muhammad 'Ali treacherously massacred the many thousands of remaining Mamluks, who posed the only possible challenge to his power. In 1826 Sultan Mahmud II solved his own problem with the janissaries in the same manner. He had them slaughtered.

For almost two decades, Egypt acted as an enforcer for the sultan. Between 1811 and 1818 Muhammad 'Ali's son Ibrahim Pasha recovered Arabia for Mahmud from the desert warriors of Abdullah ibn Saud, who had captured Medina and Mecca. In 1824 he again came to the sultan's aid against the rebellious Greeks. But Egyptian support was never recompensed, and in 1839 Ibrahim Pasha's armies moved north against the sultan, taking the coastal towns of Palestine and Syria and advancing inexorably toward Anatolia. It was intervention by the Habsburg Empire and Britain that saved Mahmud II from his overmighty subject.

It was ironic that the Ottoman Empire, torpid for generations, had suddenly spawned two great reformers, who were bound to become rivals. Muhammad 'Ali achieved in Egypt what his theoretical master, Sultan Mahmud II in Constantinople, had failed to accomplish. Egypt became a state dictatorship driven by a talented ruling family, possessing very much the energy of the earlier successful sultans, such as Mehmed the Conqueror, Selim II, and Süleyman the Lawgiver.

In the rest of the Ottoman Empire, Sultan Mahmud II could not enforce his will with the same energy and ruthless authority that Muhammad 'Ali could apply in Egypt. No quantity of European-style new uniforms and new equipment, and no replacement of ancient turbans and robes with red fezzes and Western frock coats, could disguise the sultan's political and military weakness. The sultan's obvious inability to discipline his virtually independent governor in Albania, Ali Pasha, known as the Lion of Janina, for long made nonsense of his claim to have re-created Ottoman power. Muhammad 'Ali was always careful to preserve the illusion of the sultan's authority—even when sending his army against his master. Moreover, Cairo was far from Constantinople. Ali Pasha was much closer to the imperial capital, and his independence was much more humiliating to the proud sultan.

There was one essential difference between the two reforming rulers. Muhammad 'Ali wholeheartedly adopted the economic and industrial systems of the West, whereas his master, Sultan Mahmud, failed to accomplish any similar necessary transformation of the Ottoman structure. Egypt both provided the sultan's most powerful military asset and at the same time threatened his authority. Muhammad 'Ali knew how Western power had operated during Napoleon's invasion of Egypt, whereas the sultan only imagined Europe from books or what he learned from others. Moreover Mahmud II's task was incomparably greater than the problems posed within Egypt. Frustrated by his lack of success, he died in 1839, a bitterly disappointed man. He was succeeded by his weak and malleable young son, Abdul Mejid. With Mahmud's death, Western ambassadors became the dominant figures in Constantinople, while Europeans came in increasing numbers as tourists. Pilgrimages increased to Jerusalem and the Holy Land. This European involvement extended to banks, who made huge advances, at high rates of interest; the money was spent mostly on palaces, furniture, and upholstery from Paris and the creation of a "European" lifestyle. Unlike their ancestors a century before, who had wanted Western technology but not a Western style of life, the new Ottomans aspired to become part of Western Europe.

Thus Western ideas and aspirations extended into political life. In November 1839 a "Noble Rescript" was read out to leading Ottomans and foreign ambassadors in the Rose Pavilion of Topkapi Palace. This decree instituted a modern, European-style state by imperial order. Its ideology was promoted by a group of progressive Ottoman officials, many of whom had visited Paris or Vienna. Their aims were sincere, but they failed to appreciate the vast inertia of Ottoman tradition. Nor was it just the resistance of what was still a theocratic Islamic state. The Orthodox Greek patriarch had murmured at the reading in the Rose Pavilion that he hoped the Noble Rescript would be put away and forgotten. Ottoman reformers had always struggled against reactionaries in a ruling class, including both Muslims and Christians, who had a great deal to lose from change.

But even the modernized Ottoman state suffered from the same afflictions as its unreformed predecessor. The demands made upon it always exceeded its resources. Reform did nothing to change that situation and may even have made matters worse. Mahmud II took huge pride in his Westernized regiments. He usually wore a European-style uniform like those of the European emperors of Russia and the Habsburg Empire. But he had to call in the Egyptians to suppress the Greek rebels in the 1820s, and when the Egyptians turned against him in the 1830s, they easily trounced Mahmud's new model army.

For all their empire's apparent might, the Ottomans had always governed with very scanty resources. This worked because after 1700 Ottoman governments did little beyond collecting taxes and trying vainly to suppress banditry. But the military (and, hence, the financial) pressures were increasing. The greatest threat to the Ottoman Empire was the expanding aspirations of Russia in the Black Sea and the Balkans. On two previous occasions, Russia had beaten the Ottoman armies with ease. Tsar Nicholas I began to talk of the Ottoman Empire as the "sick man of Europe" and suggested that the European powers should be making plans to dismember it. But in 1853 the Ottoman Army attacked the tsar's troops and, against all the odds, beat them. Finally, it seemed, Mahmud II's military reforms had delivered. When France and Britain joined the Ottoman side, the Crimean War ended in a major defeat for Russia's territorial ambitions.

Now, as the Ottoman Empire became a member of the small circle of European states—albeit the least powerful member—the Ottoman reformers felt secure in their state's Western destiny. But this new role carried seeds of future disaster. The empire, however much it aspired to modernity, had changed only superficially. Its political attitudes and practices remained rooted in the past, and its behavior often seemed medieval in its cruelty. Not that the Western European powers could always justify their posture of moral superiority. Britain put down the Indian Mutiny (1857) with extraordinary brutality; the Habsburg Empire showed excessive harshness toward the Hungarian revolutionaries in 1848–49, as did the French army toward the revolutionary communards of Paris in 1871.

APING THE EUROPEAN WORLD had come at a huge cost, and the massive loans made to the empire for armaments and high living also carried a political price. Ultimately, these debts were unsustainable. The Ottoman Empire was forced to default on its obligations in 1875, and Western creditors pressed their governments to set up an international commission to recover what was owed to them. Soon foreigners were micromanaging the Ottoman economy, telling farmers they had to grow tobacco instead of wheat, because that would speed up redemption of the international debt. The Ottoman government was seen to have borrowed irresponsibly, and gradually its reforming credentials were questioned in every area. One key area was Lebanon, where both France and Britain had competing interests. From 1846 to 1860, the complex internal politics of three religious communities, Druze, Christian, and Muslim, led to intracommunal strife, for which the Ottoman government was censured. They were condemned again for not preventing the massacre of Christians in Damascus in 1860, and blamed afresh for the harsh reprisals that they took against the massacre's perpetrators. The whole episode seemed to justify the critics' view that the empire was incompetent and sadistic in more or less equal mea-sure. This view became general after what were termed the Bulgarian Horrors of 1877, when thousands were killed in Bulgaria, mostly by the Ottoman militia known as *bashi bazouks*.

The killings—first in Greece in the 1820s, followed by more in the Levant and Damascus, and then in the Balkans in the 1870s —had one factor in common. They were an example more of Ottoman weakness than of an uncontrollable blood lust, as their enemies in the West claimed. Turkish power was ruthless, but its purges were deliberate and systematic, not random. There is little evidence that in the 19th century the Ottoman state supported ethnic or religious killings divorced from a political context. There was no pattern of state-sponsored pogroms of Jews or local Christians in the Middle East. What Ottoman governments and officials feared most was sedition and insurrection. It was an attitude that went back to the foundation of the state in the 15th century. Their response was instinctive and visceral: If sedition was not nipped in the bud, they would pay with their own lives. In that sense, their response to the Balkan Slavs at the beginning of the 19th century, to the Greek revolution in the 1820s, to the warring local notables in Lebanon and Damascus in the 1860s, and to the few Bulgarian revolutionaries in 1877 was the same. They used state terror to bludgeon them into submission. A later Ottoman generation responded with exactly the same unquestioning savagery to those whom they regarded as Cretan or Armenian "terrorists."

But even supposedly more "civilized" states—such as Britain, France, Austria-Hungary, and imperial Germany—sometimes behaved in broadly the same manner in the course of their colonial or national expansion. The difference was that the West regarded the Ottomans as irredeemably and culturally barbaric, whereas their own atrocities were an undesirable consequence of cruel and exceptional necessity.

IN 1876 A SLIGHTLY BUILT YOUNG MAN AGE 34 was enthroned as Sultan Abdul Hamid II. No one had expected him to become the ruler. But his uncle, Abdul Aziz, had been deposed by his ministers and then "committed suicide" in mysterious circumstances. His elder brother, Murad V, had gone mad. Abdul Hamid came to the throne reluctantly, but in the end he reigned for 33 years. Many of his predecessors had been labeled as insane, vicious, and lustful, but Abdul Hamid was none of these. He has gone down in history, however, as Abdul the Damned, whose hands were stained red with the blood of his victims. In his old age the sultan became so morbidly suspicious that he locked himself away in a hilltop palace, surrounded by thousands of guards. He never slept in the same room on two successive nights, and always had a pistol by his hand. He was, in the eyes of his innumerable critics, craven, duplicitous, irresolute, and paranoid. Perhaps, but he also possessed political skills and ingenuity of his great ancestors.

He was also an autocrat who dispensed with the trappings of constitutional modernity that had developed under his father, Abdul Mejid, and his uncle, Abdul Aziz. He agreed to a new constitution in 1876, but Abdul Hamid was not temperamentally suited to working with a parliament. He dismissed it with the statement that "the current situation was not suitable for it properly to perform its functions." The situation never was, in his eyes, "suitable." After the Congress of Berlin in 1878 reconstructed the Balkans, he had to accept a dramatic loss of Ottoman territory, and not only in Europe. More humiliations were to follow. Bosnia and Herzegovina were occupied by Austria-Hungary. Tunisia was forced to accept French "protection" in 1881 and was lost. The British took control of Egypt in 1882. Yet these were mostly lands where the Ottomans could claim at best a theoretical sovereignty. Egypt remained in theory and legally an Ottoman province, as did Bosnia and Herzegovina until 1908. The empire ruled by Abdul Hamid II after 1885 was different from the old empire built by his ancestors. For the first time the Middle East and Anatolia rather than southwestern Europe or North Africa were its prime constituents.

Abdul Hamid was autocratic but not a fossilized and mindless reactionary. He himself said, "I made a mistake when I wished to imitate my father Abdul Mejid, who sought to reform by persuasion.... I shall follow in the footsteps of my grandfather Sultan Mahmud. Like him I now understand that it is only by force that one can move the people with whose protection God has entrusted me." Like his grandfather he wanted to use the attributes of modernity but not to adopt its spirit. He welcomed the railroads and paved highways, the telegraph and the telephone. He decreed a comprehensive system of education and, more eccentrically, pioneered the use of the camera as a means of documenting events, sending photographers throughout his lands to become the sultan's eyes.

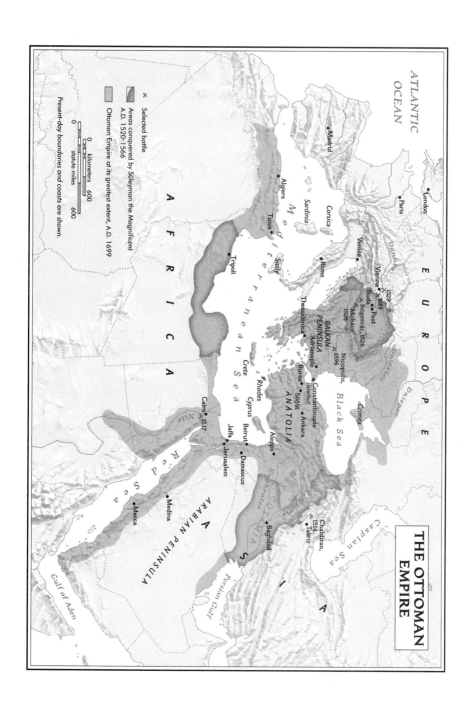

THE OTTOMAN EMPIRE

ATLANTIC
OCEAN

× Selected battle

Areas conquered by Süleyman the Magnificent
A.D. 1520-1566

Ottoman Empire at its greatest extent, A.D. 1699

0   kilometers   600

0   statute miles   600

Present-day boundaries and coasts are shown.

London
Paris
Madrid

EUROPE

Mediterranean Sea

Algiers
Sardinia
Corsica
Tunis
Sicily
Rome
Venice
Tripoli

Danube

Vienna ×1529
Buda ×1683
Pest
× Szigetvár, 1526
× Mohács,
1526

BALKAN
PENINSULA
Adrianople
× Nicopolis,
1396

Thessalonica

Crete
Rhodes
Cyprus

Bursa
Söğüt
Istanbul
Constantinople

Black Sea

Crimea

ANATOLIA
Ankara

AFRICA

Nile

Cairo
×1517

Jaffa
Jerusalem
Beirut
Damascus
Aleppo

Red Sea

Medina
Mecca

ARABIAN PENINSULA

MESOPOTAMIA

Euphrates
Tigris

Baghdad

×1514
Tabriz
Chaldiran,

Caspian Sea

ASIA

Persian Gulf

Gulf of Aden

The Ottoman Age   61

Thousands of images were sent back to the Yildiz Palace in Istanbul, where the sultan pored over them. He supplemented these images with reports from his efficient intelligence system. Abdul Hamid was one of the better informed rulers in the 19th century. In his empire, the palace of Yildiz was the center of the Ottoman world, as the Topkapi had been in earlier centuries.

This palace government was entirely in the Ottoman tradition established by Mehmed the Conqueror. It was the sultan who personally managed the complex imperial debt and devised new forms of taxation beyond those sources already committed by treaty to paying off international loans. Abdul Hamid wanted to tax every sheep traded, and most sales of real property. He increased the tithe paid by Muslims and the military service tax paid by non-Muslims. He even tried to tax foreigners working in the Ottoman Empire, but was pressured by foreign governments into withdrawing the decree. Resentful of the pressures and controls instituted by the European powers, Abdul Hamid enlarged the Islamic credentials of his state, which played very well among many of his subjects in the Middle East. He invested considerable sums in mosques, religious education, and salaries for Islamic teachers. The sultan wanted to give Arabic an equivalent status to Ottoman Turkish as an official language of state but was eventually dissuaded by his officials. Nonetheless, many Arabs from Syria, Lebanon, Jerusalem, and Iraq came to serve in his administration. He sponsored the building of a railroad south from Damascus to the holy city of Medina, thereby making the pilgrimage to Mecca a much easier, safer, and cheaper prospect. This was paid for partly by the sultan from his private resources but mostly from contributions made by devout Muslims. The sultan's standing rose very high throughout the Muslim world.

Yet by the 1890s there was also evidence of a system in decay. In 1896 Armenian revolutionaries seized the Ottoman Bank (Banque Ottomane, founded 1863) in Pera, the European quarter of Constantinople. This was a symbolic act designed to signal the impotence of the imperial government. Abdul Hamid considered it pure terrorism. Savage repression of Armenians in the traditional Ottoman style proved completely ineffectual. Responding to inept revolutionary terror with random state terror simply did not work. The sultan's failure to solve the problem of sedition, by both Armenians and Macedonians within the empire, turned the Ottoman Army to more radical steps. In Damascus in 1905 a young officer called Mustafa Kemal was founding a secret society called Fatherland (Vatan), with cells in the garrisons of Jerusalem and Jaffa. He took his political agenda to the Third Army, stationed in Macedonia, where it rapidly took root. Kemal, who inspired the transformation of the Ottoman Empire, later became much better known as Atatürk, the Father of the Turks, who created the new nation of Turkey after World War I.

The large group of radicals in the army made contact with Ottoman political exiles in Paris, and together they prepared a common program. Their stated aim was not to overthrow the sultan but to restore the parliament last called in 1878. Faced with a military revolt, in July 1908 Abdul Hamid trumped their ace by recalling parliament, saying with great bravado that it had always been his intention that it should meet again. So, in 1908 Abdul Hamid became once more a constitutional monarch governing with the help of a parliament. He was only playing for time. After less than a year, the wily sultan supported a counterrevolution, which took control of the capital. But the coup d'état failed and Abdul Hamid II was deposed. The army replaced him with his younger brother as Mehmed V. In 1909 the old sultan was exiled to Salonica (now Thessaloniki) until 1912, when he was brought back to Istanbul lest he fall into the hands of the enemy during the Balkan Wars of 1912–13. He spent the last years of his life in seclusion in the Beylerbey Palace overlooking the Bosporus, dying in 1918.

Although the rule of the Ottoman sultan officially continued until the abolition of the sultanate in 1922, it ceased to have any political reality after the exile of Abdul Hamid II. It is idle to speculate what Abdul Hamid, in his final years at Beylerbey, thought of his successors and their competence. He read the newspapers every day and was always avid for news of the war. But he did once say of the empire's defeats: "How is this possible? It is madness." Ottoman sultans were always conscious of their patrimony and the need to pass on an inheritance to future generations. There was an Ottoman ideology or myth that went back to the days of Osman I. Over the centuries, caution rather than imprudence had governed their politics. For this reason, rightly, outsiders had thought of the empire as conservative and unwilling to change. But this was not entirely so. There were many Ottoman modernizers, Abdul Hamid among them. In the Middle East there was little resentment of the sultans, who ruled by the grace of God. They did not suppress the growing national ambitions of the few Arabs interested in political issues but rather co-opted them within the Ottoman system.

It was Abdul Hamid's supplanters who were emotionally committed to a state with a stronger Turkish character. Lawrence of Arabia later wrote that "they set themselves to stamp out all non-Turkish currents in the State, especially Arab and Armenian 'nationalism.'" One of those who deposed the sultan, Jamal Pasha, executed numerous Arab nationalists in 1915. His act is remembered with bitterness to this day. Some of the other new leaders, especially Talat and Enver Pasha, found their political inspiration in imperial Germany, but Mustafa Kemal (later Atatürk) did not. He looked to the Turkish past for the source of his inspiration. His model was Mehmed the Conqueror. All this, of course, was in the future, after a World War had destroyed the Ottoman hold on the Middle East. Under Kemal the new Turkey would withdraw into Anatolia and find solace in its Turkish heritage. All claims over the old empire below the Anatolian plateau would be abandoned, both for the territory and in terms of any cultural inheritance. The Arabic script and literature would be spurned, Turkey would become a secular state, officially abandoning Islam as a state religion. The Western world would become the model for future progress. Symbolically, the fez would be abandoned for a European trilby.

The new leaders would also turn their back on the old capital. Eighty-six Byzantine emperors, seven Latin rulers, and thirty Ottoman sultans had ruled from the city of Constantine. It has been calculated that it had more than a hundred names and nicknames, in Latin, Greek, Arabic, Turkish, and other vernaculars of the empire, paying tribute to its power and grandeur. Since 1453 the city had represented continuity and stability, and even in the 19th and 20th centuries it was capable of inspiring fear and respect within the Ottoman domains. After the World War, French and British rule largely replaced the Turks in the Middle East, but their rule had rather a temporary feel. The dusty new Turkish capital in a sleepy provincial town called Angora (Ankara) had no imperial tradition. So what emerged after the end of Ottoman rule was a political void, only partly to be filled by new national identities. No one was nostalgic for Ottoman rule. It is only recently that the Turks themselves have begun to appreciate their Ottoman past, and no one else has any affection for the old imperial days. But the lack of an overarching political and economic structure embracing much of the Middle East, which had existed for more than four centuries under the Ottomans, has resulted in strife and human suffering on a grand scale.

In the early 20th century, a new form of transportation, double-decked, horse-drawn streetcars on rails, drew curious stares from travelers on the road to Baghdad.

CHAPTER FOUR

1914 TO 1920

END OF AN AGE, BIRTH OF CONFLICT

DAVID FROMKIN

ON JANUARY 3, 1914, A YOUNG OFFICER NAMED ENVER—
Enver Pasha, to give him his honorific title—took office as minister of war
of the Ottoman Empire. He was 32 years old at the time. A vain man who
gloried in uniforms and medals and theatrical gestures, he had caught the
public's imagination by riding on a white charger through the streets of
an undefended city in the Second Balkan War the year before. He seemed
to carry all before him: He took a niece of the sultan as his wife and moved
into a palace on the Bosporus. He was, like Napoleon, noticeably short,
but he was no Napoleon when it came to political or military genius. Quite
the contrary. His generalship and his political leadership both were to
prove disastrous. It is no exaggeration to say that, had he never lived, the
Ottoman Empire might not have died—at least not when it did.

Enver was a leader of the Committee of Union and Progress—the
C.U.P., or Young Turkey Party. The Young Turks were "new men," self-made
and lacking family background. They had surfaced in Turkish politics in
1908, and by the end of 1913 had finally succeeded in pushing aside the

old guard: the established figures, the notables, and the aristocracy.

Although Enver was the Young Turks' charismatic public figure, its paramount leader—its inside power—was Mehmet Talat, who took office as minister of the interior. Rumored to be of gypsy blood, he was hawk-nosed, had thick black hair and heavy eyebrows, and, in the words of a British traveler in Turkish lands, possessed "a light in his eyes, rarely seen in men but sometimes in animals at dusk." Talat had a gift for organization that was of special value in the environment, where political groups and freedom of expression were repressed and societies that survived were of necessity secret. Reputed to be a dervish and a Mason, Talat, as an employee of the Post and Telegraph Office, was a master of the cable network and could honeycomb the empire for his Young Turks movement more effectively than any rival secret societies.

Talat recruited a key senior military figure, Ahmed Jamal Pasha. Jamal, who became the third main leader of the C.U.P. Young army officers formed the backbone of the secret societies in the Ottoman Empire at that time, and Jamal, a staff officer of the Ottoman Third Army headquartered in Macedonia, became a liaison to probably the largest group of disaffected soldiers in the empire: young men conscious that a backward society and inept leaders had doomed them to lose a province they were capable of holding. A wild, lawless province on the disappearing Ottoman Balkan frontier, coveted by neighboring states, Macedonia also proved to be outside the reach of the sultan's political police. It was a revolt in Macedonia that first brought the Young Turks to the fore.

By 1914 the C.U.P. was securely in power in Constantinople, the Ottoman capital. The sultan had been reduced to a mere figurehead. Courtly Prince Said Halim provided a respectable face to the outside world as grand vizier and foreign minister. The empire was ruled, however, by the central committee of the C.U.P. and the C.U.P.-dominated cabinet.

Pressing questions, postponed for far too long, demanded immediate responses from the new government. One of these was the nationalities question. There was no Ottoman nationality; instead the empire comprised roughly two dozen peoples, preserving languages and cultures of their own. Who should rule? On its road to power, the Young Turkey Party had promised that each of the empire's peoples would have a fair participation in the government and that there would be a multinational government for a multinational state. Once securely in power, however, the C.U.P., overwhelmingly Turkish-speaking, opted not to share. The roughly 40 percent of the empire's population who spoke Turkish would continue to rule the 40 percent who spoke Arabic and the remaining 20 percent who spoke some other language.

As commanders of their country's forces, the new men were aware that their situation was precarious. The Ottoman armies had been in a long retreat since the end of the 17th century. Their most recent losses in the Italian and Balkan wars had been nearly fatal. By 1914 they were down to manning their last—their inner—lines of defense.

To protect their domains, at least for the short run, the Young Turks needed support from one of the great powers of Europe. But as one after another of the powers was sounded out informally by Turkish leaders, they declined to help. The Europeans were not ill disposed to propping up the empire—on the contrary, Britain and France had personal stakes in its continuation. In order to maintain regional stability, Britain, for example, had supported the Ottomans in the past and still wanted the empire's disintegration postponed for as long as possible. And France, whose investors in large part financed the Ottoman public debt, had a huge monetary stake in the empire's continued existence. But no European state wanted to commit to defend the existing Ottoman frontiers against predatory Italy or against the ferocious, hungry new Christian states of the Balkans, backed, it was feared, by the Russian colossus.

The last of the European countries to be approached was Germany. At a secret meeting at the villa of the grand vizier in July 1914, key C.U.P. leaders authorized Enver to make the approach. Enver had served in Berlin and maintained good connections to the German capital. He made his approach July 22 and was turned down immediately by the German ambassador in Constantinople. But Europe was in a state of crisis, and the German emperor, Kaiser Wilhelm II, personally intervened to send his country's ambassador to the conference table. By August 2 the secret talks were concluded with a straightforward German guarantee: "Germany obligates itself, by force of arms if need be, to defend Ottoman territory in case it should be threatened."

What Turkey pledged in return was not so clear. The Ottoman Empire promised to fight side by side with Germany, but only against Russia and only in defined circumstances, which may or may not have occurred when the Great War broke out in Europe in August 1914. Specifically, Turkey had to go to war if Germany was required to come to Austria's aid. But if Austria started the war (as many now believe), it was less clear that Germany (and therefore Turkey) had to intervene. Even if the secret Germany-Turkey treaty were interpreted to mean that Turkey was obligated to enter the war on Germany's side, no provision was made for when it had to do so. For a state as unready for modern warfare as was the Ottoman Empire in mid-1914, that was a significant omission.

Only Enver, Talat, the grand vizier, and a few trusted colleagues were aware that an alliance had been concluded, and it became evident almost immediately that remaining on the sidelines in the war held powerful advantages for the Turks. The Allies, who did not know of the secret Turkish-German alliance, wooed Turkey in their turn. Indeed, they were prepared to offer a great deal—notably a guarantee of continued existence—if Turkey would remain neutral. Events at sea soon made neutrality even more attractive.

WHEN HOSTILITIES COMMENCED IN EUROPE during the first days of August 1914, the powerful German battleship *Goeben*, accompanied by the light cruiser *Breslau*, found itself in the western Mediterranean, off French North Africa. The Allied navies of England and France were seemingly supreme in the Mediterranean, and the British Admiralty ordered its forces to hunt down and destroy the German intruders. Instead of steaming west, past Gibraltar to the open Atlantic, the German warships eluded their pursuers and raced east. Disregarding orders from Berlin and Constantinople not to do so, the *Goeben* and *Breslau* sought refuge in Turkish waters, where Enver saw to it that they were guided through the local minefields.

To turn the German warships away would be to send them to certain death, since the formidable British Mediterranean squadron was in close pursuit. At one in the morning of August 6, the grand vizier, Prince Said Halim, discussed the situation with the German ambassador, Hans von Wangenheim. The grand vizier announced that his government would allow the vessels to stay but that there would be a price. The terms were stiff. The Turks advanced six proposals, among them the abolition of the capitulations as regarded Germany. These treaty provisions gave the dominant European powers special privileges in the Ottoman domains.

On August 9 the grand vizier raised Turkey's terms. To provide sanctuary for the warships would violate the international law of neutrality, so Germany (argued Said Halim) should give the *Goeben* and the *Breslau* to Turkey as a gift. Von Wangenheim refused. Whereupon the Ottoman government publicly announced that it had bought and paid for the warships and now owned them. Joyous crowds celebrated in the streets of Constantinople. On August 14 a frustrated von Wangenheim advised Berlin that there was no alternative but to go along with the story told by the Turks—or else public opinion would turn against Germany.

Lacking the naval officers and crews to man such sophisticated modern vessels, the Turks gave the German captain and his men fezzes and Ottoman uniforms and swore them into the Turkish Navy.

On September 8, 1914, the Ottoman government announced its unilateral abrogation of the capitulation treaties and privileges of all foreign powers—including Germany. All of the countries affected objected, of course, but to no avail. The Young Turks government had taken a giant step on the road to achieving its nationalist program.

Throughout August, September, and October of 1914, Germany brought all the pressure that it could to bear upon the Ottoman Empire to enter the war. The Turks resisted. But Enver, for reasons of his own, changed his mind and determined to bring the Ottoman Empire into the war. Apparently he had come to believe that Germany was bound to win the war; and he was prepared to bet the very existence of the empire that he was right.

The murky details of Enver's intrigues still are not completely known to historians. By the end of October, however, he had concluded that he could not carry a majority in the C.U.P. central committee to adopt a war policy. Instead, he would have to force his country's hand.

Working with the minister of the marine, he arranged for the *Goeben* and *Breslau,* now christened the *Sultan Selim* and the *Medilli,* to escape into the Black Sea. Once there, in their guise as Turkish vessels and flying the

Turkish flag, they bombarded the Russian coast, provoking a response from Russia and its allies that brought the Ottoman Empire into the war.

In the Allied countries, it was assumed that Turkey thereby had signed its own death warrant. The fate of its two dozen or so peoples became an immediate rather than a distant concern. What had been dreams became possibilities. In an open letter published immediately in the press, the English novelist and social thinker H. G. Wells asked, "What is to prevent the Jews having Palestine and restoring a real Judaea?" Jews were not the only ones; for Armenians, Asia Minor Greeks, and others, Enver had opened a window of opportunity for each to restore its individual autonomy on soil that, until 1914, had been controlled by the Ottoman Empire.

It did not occur to Allied leaders that the backward Ottoman Empire posed any kind of military threat. The initial campaigns launched by Turkey seemed to confirm that judgment. At the end of December 1914, Enver personally led an attack on the Russian Caucasus that collapsed in a matter of weeks. He lost an estimated 85,000 of his 100,000 troops. A German officer who was attached to the Ottoman general staff reported that Enver's forces had "suffered a disaster which for rapidity and completeness is without parallel in military history." Immediately afterward, Jamal led a Turkish attack on the Suez Canal that resulted in a complete rout for the Ottoman forces.

But in 1915–16, the tide of battle turned. British India mounted an invasion of what is now Iraq and got almost as far as Baghdad before being turned back by Ottoman forces led by a German field marshal. The British forces were destroyed in the course of a retreat and subsequent siege, leaving them few survivors.

At about the same time Allied naval forces, and later Allied army forces, attacked the Dardanelles in a campaign whose details are disputed still. Throwing away one opportunity of winning after another, the Allied fleet turned around and steamed away from the Dardanelles, and the Allied land forces evacuated the beaches of the Gallipoli Peninsula 259 days after landing on them, after they and the Turks each had suffered a quarter million casualties. For the Allies, it was a tragedy, for the Ottoman Empire, a triumph, in which the battlefield genius of a Turkish officer, Mustafa Kemal, at last had a chance to shine.

But then the tides of battle turned again as Great Britain's dynamic new prime minister, David Lloyd George, focused more closely on defeating and destroying the Ottoman Empire. In December 1916, as Lloyd George was taking office, British India once again invaded what is now Iraq and by mid-March had captured Baghdad. Later that year the British expeditionary force based in Egypt attacked and took first Palestine, then Syria the following year.

In the north of what now is Turkey a half million or so Russian troops poured across the frontier, and might well have won the war if the Russian Revolution of 1917 had not brought them to a halt. As Russia then disintegrated, Enver recklessly sent his remaining troops north in a futile effort to carve a new empire out of the tsar's domains that would compensate for the empire of the sultans he was in the process of losing in the south.

By the autumn of 1918, having learned that Germany planned to surrender, the Young Turks government in Constantinople decided to do so also. On October 30, aboard the British battleship *Agamemnon,* anchored off the Greek island of Lemnos, the Ottoman peace delegation signed an armistice of surrender that recognized the empire's loss of its Arab-speaking provinces. Three days later, Enver, Talat, and Jamal, the main Young Turk leaders, fled with their German allies to seek hiding places in Europe. Mehmed VI, who had become sultan only months before on the death of his brother, awaited news of his fate, apparently prepared to make any concessions that would allow him to keep his throne.

As the armistice required, the Ottoman authorities demobilized their armed forces, except those required to keep order in Turkey. The troops stacked their weapons and piled up their munitions in dumps. British officers rode through the countryside to supervise. The Arab-speaking areas of the empire would remain mostly under British military administration.

THROUGHOUT THE WAR, THE ALLIES HAD discussed how the Ottoman Empire should be divided after it ended. They had even entered into treaties, all of them secret and some of doubtful validity. There were many peoples and governments asserting claims and arguing that they had been promised or allowed to believe that such claims would be honored.

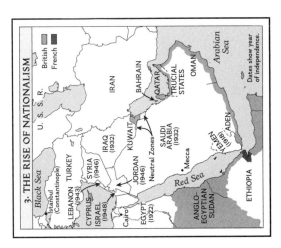

3. THE RISE OF NATIONALISM

British French

Dates show year of independence.

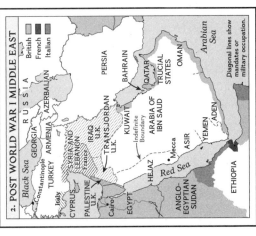

2. POST WORLD WAR I MIDDLE EAST

British French Italian

Diagonal lines show mandates or military occupation.

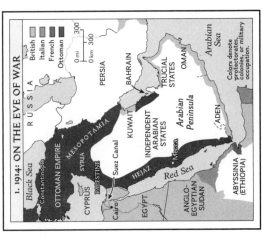

1. 1914: ON THE EVE OF WAR

British Italian French Ottoman

0 mi 300
0 km 300

Colors denote protectorates, colonies, or military occupation.

Three realities, in particular, determined the course of events in the years that immediately followed. The first was that the British occupation force of a million men in the lands of the Ottoman Empire was the only significant armed force in the Middle East. That meant that anything Britain wanted to have done was likely to be done, so long as this situation continued. The second reality was the converse of the first. As War Minister Winston Churchill told the prime minister in 1919, "Unless we are to be defrauded of the fruits of victory and ... to throw away all that we have won ... we must provide for a good many months to come Armies of Occupation for the enemy's territory. These armies must be strong enough to extract from ... the Turks and others" the terms Britain wished to impose. Or, as Churchill told the House of Commons, "Do not disband your army until you have got your terms." But his advice was not heeded. The domestic political pressure for demobilization was too great. By October 19 Churchill admitted that "the Army had melted away."

The third reality, related to the above two, was that the passage of time brings with it change: What can be done today may not be doable next year. So it was with the Ottoman Empire. As the victorious Allies chose to deal with the defeated countries separately, and as quarrels prevented quick agreement on the Middle East, the treaty with the Ottomans was the last of all to be drafted. Agreement was still reachable on the Arab-speaking half of the empire.

For centuries, European leaders had wondered how they would divide up the Middle East once the Ottoman Empire disappeared. Now the time for decision had arrived. France took Syria and later spun off Lebanon from it. Great Britain took Palestine and the provinces of Baghdad, Basra, and Mosul, which it merged into a new state to be called Iraq. This division of the Arab-speaking Middle East between Britain and France followed roughly the lines of a secret agreement reached by the Allies during the war.

The Turkish-speaking center of the Ottoman Empire was another matter. One possibility was simply to wipe Turkey off the map. By August 10, 1920, when the Allies imposed upon the sultan's government the Treaty of Sèvres, emasculating what remained of the Turkish-speaking Ottoman domains, the life had gone out of the sultan's state. Turks in the interior had rallied to the nationalist leader, Mustafa Kemal, the hero of Gallipoli.

An Allied-sanctioned landing on May 15, 1919, of Greek troops on the Turkish coast was the first step in a war that would continue sporadically through 1922. In it Greece and a nascent Turkish republic fought savagely, and the Ottoman Empire, already a ghost, played no role. It had disappeared from history. On October 10, 1922, the Armistice of Mudanya marked Kemal's victory over the Allies and Greece, but also over the Ottoman past. The Ottoman Sultanate was formally abolished by the Turkish Assembly on November 1, 1922. The Ottoman Empire had endured for nearly five centuries. Enver Pasha had gambled it away in less than five years.

In deference to the rising force of public opinion, and to the anti-imperialist rhetoric in both the United States and the Soviet Union, the two allies held their respective shares of the Arabic-speaking Middle East in the form of "mandates" from the League of Nations—temporary trusteeships of states designed to become self-governing and fully independent when capable of that, be it sooner or later. It was a formula bound to cause strife in the years to come, as local leaders demanded that freedom come sooner and Britain and France insisted that it come later.

THE ALLIES WERE CRITICIZED throughout this period for having made secret wartime promises—and also for not keeping those promises. But this was not entirely justified legally: Britain had carefully drafted the language of its pledges, especially those to the Arabs, so as to suggest full support from London while legally committing the British to nothing. Negotiating peace terms while the war was still raging proved to be a murky business. In dealing with the British, those who purported to represent the Arab world—Sharif Hussein, the Turkish-appointed emir, and a young deserter from the Ottoman Army named Muhammad Al-Faruqi—had no right to do so. They had no following and could speak only for themselves. They allowed British intelligence to believe that hundreds of thousands of Arab troops in the Ottoman Army would come over to the Allied side—which seems to have been a fantasy or a fabrication—if their terms were met. These included a promise from Britain that after the war all of Arab-speaking western Asia would be united in a single, independent kingdom. British officials expressed sympathy for this goal but subjected it to qualifications that essentially took back everything they had appeared to give.

Agreement was never reached among the parties to these disputes, and in the end neither side delivered what the other had asked for. The British thereafter escalated the obfuscation, first telling Arab leaders that their demands for a unified kingdom could not be met because France had the prior claim, then telling France that Britain could not honor promises to it regarding a Greater Syria because the Arabs had a superior claim. Thus the peace terms, when finally arrived at, were a product of bad faith.

In drawing a new map of the Middle East, the Allies have been criticized repeatedly for creating boundaries and designing new countries to suit their own needs and desires rather than those of the people who lived there. For these reasons, and perhaps others as well, a sense of illegitimacy has hovered about the Middle Eastern peace settlement of 1918 to 1922. Eighty years later, the question of Ottoman succession still has not been completely resolved. Will Kurdistan or Palestine become countries? Will Lebanon free itself of Syria? Will Israel continue to survive?

Ironically, it is still too soon to say what the final outcome of the Ottoman Empire's dissolution will be.

With a backdrop of Arabic grafitti proclaiming "Jerusalem Is Ours," a Palestinian youth hurls a rock at Israeli soldiers, pitching the area's continuous strife into the 21st century.

CHAPTER FIVE

1920 TO 2002

CENTURY OF STRIFE

SANDRA MACKEY

WHEN THE SUN BROKE ON THE NEW YEAR OF 1920, ITS RAYS descended on a Middle East that had been forever altered by the collapse of the Ottoman Empire. In Istanbul, Topkapi Palace, the magnificent seat of the Ottoman caliph, clung to a hill above the Bosporus, little more than a symbol of dissolution. Power had moved elsewhere—to Kemal Atatürk, who would lift Turkey out of a fallen empire built on Islam and drive it toward secularism and westernization. To the east, Iran was creeping out from the shadow that the Ottomans had cast over Persia for 400 years. With the Qajar dynasty metaphorically on its deathbed, Reza Khan, a charismatic military figure, was poised to found the Pahlavi dynasty, which would rule Iran until the 1979 Islamic revolution. Both the Turks and the Persians were moving into their changed world as people possessing a deep sense of who they were. Although they would not escape the conflicts of identity and the challenges of modernization that stretched out before them, each society was securely anchored by its past and held together by authentic nationalism. But in the heart of the Middle East, the Arabs of the fallen Ottoman Empire possessed no such identity as a distinct people with a defined territory carved out by common history. Instead, the Arabs—the vast majority of the population of the Middle East— were largely an amalgam of families and tribes, divided psychologically between the urban attitudes of the city and the traditions of the country and physically split between the Fertile Crescent (a semicircle of fertile land stretching from the southeast coast of the Mediterranean around the Syrian Desert north of the Arabian Peninsula to the Persian Gulf) and the wastelands of the Arabian Peninsula. With the exception of the Egyptians, who felt an emotional attachment to their ancient past, and the scattered people of the Arabian Peninsula, who prided themselves on their Bedouin heritage, Arab identity resided in a common language that gave to both Muslims and non-Muslims a loose concept of Arab nationalism.

During World War I, Britain had seemed to promise the Arabs of the Ottoman Empire a unitary state stretching from the eastern coast of the Mediterranean to the eastern bank of the Tigris River. But with peace, the Arabs became citizens of a series of contrived states named Syria, Transjordan, Palestine, and Iraq, whose boundaries were drawn to meet the imperial needs of the war's victorious allies—Britain and France. In newly defined Palestine, the Arabs faced not only European colonialism but the challenge of Zionism—powerful Jewish nationalism—which had arrived from Europe in the late 19th century. Through the rest of the 20th century and into the 21st, the Arabs from the Nile to the Tigris, from the mountains of northern Iraq to the tip of Yemen, have struggled to find independence, identity, political stability, and social justice. Yet what they have experienced is foreign occupation, conflicted concepts of identity, splintered societies, political turmoil, repressive regimes, and economic disparity. Intertwined with their inability either to confront successfully or to find accommodation with Israel, the Arabs' quest for identity, progress, and justice has largely written the contemporary history of the Middle East. The wide, convoluted lines the Arabs have followed in search of themselves are labeled nationalism, socialism, and Islam.

Over the 500 years when most of the Middle East belonged to the Ottoman Empire, the Arabs rarely thought of themselves in terms of territory. Identity came out of language and kinship defined by precise genealogies. As victims of conquering armies that for centuries marched back and forth across the Fertile Crescent and then as subjects of the Ottoman Empire, who were tied to Istanbul by little but Islam, the Arabs developed no concept of the nation-state built on the Western model.

Nevertheless, at the end of World War I, the Arabs of the Fertile Crescent were segmented and then jammed into contrived states containing a hodgepodge of different sectarian and ethnic groups that separated themselves further into families and tribes. On the Arabian Peninsula, the territories that were ruled by tribal leaders stayed locked into varying relationships with Britain. And Egypt remained as it had been since 1882—a protectorate, or vassal state, of imperial Britain. Only Saudi Arabia became an independent state. Isolated and abjectly poor, it survived on a stipend from London.

In order to put a face of legality on what was really outright colonialism, the fledgling League of Nations designated Syria, Iraq, Transjordan, and Palestine as mandates. Each was assigned to France or Britain, which were charged, at least theoretically, with preparing the territory and its people for independence. In two of these mandates—Transjordan and Iraq—Britain constructed thrones and placed on them the sons of the Sharif of Mecca, the leader of the Arab Revolt and the man who had been expected to rule the great unified Arab state. The king of Egypt, whose ancestors had come from Albania, continued to rule under the tutelage of Britain.

Thus, fragile regimes controlled by European masters undertook the task of government. Each of these territories had been left by the Ottomans with little in the way of governmental experience, physical infrastructure, public education, or social services. As a result, they lacked the most basic resources needed to begin the critical process of nation building that would draw people rooted in family, tribe, religion, and sect into a society sharing common values and goals. Even so, leaders, chosen largely by the mandatory authorities, picked up the reins of their contrived states to drive them toward nationhood and modernization.

For the most part, these leaders installed at the heads of governments were reformers who saw the modernization of their societies in much the same way as the mandatory powers did—political, economic, and social mirrors of Western Europe. To their credit, some realized that the future of their frail states depended, in part, on education. But no matter how commendable the exercise, the rapid expansion of public education during the 1920s and 1930s created unanticipated problems. Because of the combination of a cultural bias against manual labor and the esoteric tradition of learning within Islam, which focused on Islamic law and Arabic language and literary traditions, the new school systems educated students for the professions or prepared them for government service, ignoring the technical and vocational training that would produce the skilled labor required for economic development. No less important, public education further segmented populations already lacking a common identity beyond the sense of being Arab. The lower classes learned in state schools, where students acquired all their knowledge and perceptions through the Arabic language; the elite educated their children in private schools. Taught in English or French, they inched outside the boundaries of Arabic-Islamic tradition. As a result, the distance between the traditionalists of the lower classes and the modernizers of the middle and upper classes grew intellectually. It also expanded physically.

In the cities, the notables and bourgeoisie, the craftsmen and shopkeepers had lived side by side for centuries in a social system based on shared values, customs, and benefits. The urbanites, in turn, were linked to those in the country through language, culture, and intertwined economies. But by the 1930s this web of belonging had begun to unravel. The upper and middle classes resided in their own areas of the city, separated from the skilled workers and shop owners by money and power and by attitudes, tastes, and habits. For much of the educated elite, Islam had come to represent an inherited culture rather than the unquestioned definition of life and ultimate symbol of community. Consequently, this elite—which was best equipped to foster a sense of nation among all citizens and to promote the economic advancement of the entire society—stood apart from the majority, who lived in burgeoning areas fed by high birthrates and waves of immigrants from the neglected, overpopulated countryside.

The one common touchstone of the haves and the have-nots of the 1920s and 1930s was the certainty that independence from their Western overlords would solve all the crushing problems of their fledgling states. Yet even the powerful desire for independence imposed its own divisions on the societies of the Fertile Crescent, principally on the elites promoting the nationalist vision. Motivated by ideology and vested interests, one strain of nationalists sought cooperation with current or former colonial masters while the other strain insisted on total separation. They found consensus only in the desire for a national army that would stabilize governments attempting to rule fractious societies. But too often the military, the promised implement of unity, became a force of politics rather than an agent of genuine nationalism.

INDEPENDENCE AND THE END OF OUTRIGHT COLONIALISM in the Fertile Crescent came with the collapse of France under the boot of Nazi Germany in 1940 and the debilitating economic problems faced by Britain after the Second World War. In 1946 Syria, Lebanon, and Jordan joined Iraq, Egypt, and Saudi Arabia as technically sovereign states. (By that time Lebanon had been split off from Syria, and Transjordan had become simply Jordan.) Having largely escaped the colonial yoke, the Arabs still found themselves engulfed by rapid change, exploding populations, swelling cities, economic stagnation, and stratifying societies. No longer able to blame their ills on foreign occupation, they were forced to confront a deep discontent with themselves and their world.

Within the intelligentsia, Arab writers explored the alienation of the individual from society and society from its rulers. Turning the village into a symbol of the man or woman hemmed in by the sterile streets of the city, the Iraqi poet Badr Shakir al-Sayyad bemoaned the dislocations of modern life: "Streets of which tales told by the fireside say, No one returns from them, as no one returns from the shore of death...."

Other poets grappled with the question of identity in an age of anxiety, and still others tilled the theme of the Arab nation and its lamentable weaknesses. To all of these writers, the Arab predicament demanded the birth of a new individual capable of creating a new Arab nation. This call for the revitalization of Arab nationalism came at a time when Arab attention concentrated on events in Palestine, the only remaining mandate, under Britain. Here the searing issue was not Arab independence from European colonialism but the Arabs' contest for territory with Jews from Europe. It was an issue that had plagued the Middle East continually for decades—and still does.

Jews returning at last to their homeland had landed on the shores of Ottoman Palestine in 1877. Beginning in 1882, more Jews began to arrive. Unlike their predecessors, who had sought nothing more than escape from the pogroms of Eastern Europe, the new arrivals bore the flame of Zionism, the passionate ideology of Jewish nationalism. During World War I the Zionists had won Britain's support, announced in the Balfour Declaration of 1917, for a homeland on the ancient stones of Palestine. The Jews achieved this unofficial pledge—though it proved hollow—in part by financing forces inside Germany that were working against the kaiser. When London assumed command of Palestine under the auspices of the League of Nations, the British government also assumed the mounting Arab-Zionist conflict. Confronted by an eruption of violence between the two communities in 1929 and again in 1936, Britain failed to find a solution to the problem of two peoples contending for the same territory. Shortly after World War II, London decided it would no longer even try. Pressured by Western guilt surrounding the Holocaust and unable to stem the migration of Jews out of Europe's displaced-persons camps, which was rapidly increasing the Jewish population of Palestine, Britain announced in February 1947 its intention to surrender the problem of Palestine to the newly founded United Nations. When the Arabs subsequently rejected a UN plan to partition Palestine between the two claimants, the Zionists declared war in the name of a Jewish state.

Burdened by the legacy of the Ottoman period and crippled by fissures in their own society, the Palestinians went into war lacking any clear vision other than an impassioned desire to drive the Zionists out. Their small guerrilla raids were not enough to thwart the well-organized Jews, united by a sacred call to statehood embroidered on the backdrop of the Holocaust. In the uneven contest, Zionist military units and operatives of what were Zionist terror groups employed force and panic to drive the Palestinians out of towns and villages, while the British Army restricted operations inside its barracks, waiting for the preannounced date marking the formal end of the mandate. When it came on May 14, 1948, British soldiers packed aboard ships that would take them home to England. At four o'clock in the afternoon of that same day, David Ben-Gurion, as the leader of the Zionists, proclaimed the state of Israel.

The following day, May 15, the Arab states of Egypt and Syria joined the war for Palestine. Lacking leadership, equipment, a unified strategy, and the support of Jordan, the Arab armies could neither win the war nor stop the pell-mell flight of the Palestinians off the coastal plain and out of Galilee. When their exodus finally ended, 700,000 Palestinians were homeless—more than 60 percent of the people of the entire society. They poured into refugee camps in Jordan, Syria, Lebanon, and Egypt's Gaza Strip. Unwelcome in countries burdened by their own enormous problems, the Palestinians became for all Arabs the burning symbol of their impotence against the West. In Arab perception, Israel, suckled on Western military, economic, and diplomatic support, stood as the new Western colonizer.

Although the tiny new state of Israel, surrounded by an implacable Arab enemy, acutely felt its vulnerability, the Arabs realized in the loss of Palestine that independence did not equal power. Thus the idea of Arab unity, which had been present among Arabs since the end of the 19th century, now took on greater urgency. In theory the Arab states, with a shared culture, mutual experience, and joint interests, possessed enough in common to achieve closer union. And in unity the Arabs would realize greater collective power for themselves. To this vision of oneness was added the idea that socialism could provide the engine of reform within societies in which all the problems of the 1920s, 1930s, and 1940s had only increased. Thus, in the 1950s Arab identity, Arab unity, and the promise of Arab economic progress came together in the person of Gamal Abdel Nasser of Egypt.

FROM THE DAY HE EMERGED INTO PUBLIC VIEW as leader of the Free Officers—who had deposed the Egyptian monarchy in a military coup on July 23, 1952—Nasser promised *al-izza wa'lkarama*, dignity and self-respect. Yet it was not until after 1954 that Nasser blossomed into a spellbinding speaker capable of arousing the Arab masses. Weaving together neoclassical Arabic with the language of the man in the street, he sent his words through millions of cheap radios across the frontiers of the Arab states. In a culture in which language is magic, Nasser reigned as the most successful Arab communicator of modern times.

Since the coup within his own country, Nasser had promoted social revolution and the abolition of social classes through state control of the means of production. Placing Egypt in the context of the Arab world and installing himself as its ordained leader, the Egyptian president sold to the rest of the Arab world the idea that redistribution of income would provide the masses with the education, housing, and health care they so desperately needed. This social reform could come only through the elimination of what Nasser proclaimed were the artificial boundaries of states within the Arab nation.

Nasser's charisma and ideology, which drove the dynamics of "Nasserism," thrust Egypt's leader forward as the champion of what the Arabs saw as their central problems beyond reform: the remaining influence of Britain and France and increasing Zionism. In 1956 Nasser attacked the vestiges of colonialism by nationalizing the British-French-owned Suez Canal. When London and Paris sent their military might to defend their property, Israel supported them. The Egyptians prevailed, not because of prowess on the battlefield but because the United States forced its allies to step down. The Americans feared that a defeated Nasser would turn to the Soviet Union and that its influence in the Middle East would increase. Keenly aware of this fear, Nasser frequently used the U.S.S.R. to intimidate the United States, thereby entangling the region in Cold War politics.

He was also a master at manipulating Arab sentiment: In the 1956 phantom Egyptian victory, Nasser took the theory and emotional appeal of Arab nationalism out of the realm of the intellectuals and gave it to the masses. Through his powerful oratory, he translated the excitement of transformation to the peasant, the laborer, and the underemployed. Seen by Arabic-speaking people from North Africa to the eastern border of Iraq as their long-awaited leader, Nasser and his priorities came to set the agenda for both his allies and his enemies. For nothing in the Middle East between 1956 and 1967 happened in isolation from Gamal Abdel Nasser.

The irony was that Nasserism came about as an accidental by-product of Nasser's successful moves and policies undertaken on behalf of Egypt's own particular national interests. His subsequent failure to create a united Arab nation through mergers between Egypt and other Arab states resulted from the reluctance of his Arab neighbors, keenly aware of their own particular interests, to subjugate themselves to Egypt. By the 1960s Arab nationalism no longer fed on the vestiges of imperial rule. Instead its ideology, as defined by Nasser, divided Arab governments between those who supported rapid change along broadly Nasserite lines and those who fought what was a difficult battle to isolate the influence of Nasserism before it destabilized the existing order in which their interests were invested. Before either of these positions could achieve dominance within the broader context of Arab politics, Nasser overreached his power, bringing all the hopes of the Arab masses crashing down in 1967.

Because United Nations peacekeeping forces had been planted on the Egypt-Israel border since the end of the 1956 Suez War, Nasser had enjoyed a decade of Arab nationalist militancy without the risk of war with Israel. But to hold his place at the head of the mythical Arab nation, the self-declared Arab messiah found himself unable to sustain "no war, no peace" with Israel forever. In a serious miscalculation, he ordered the United Nations peacekeeping forces to leave. In the ensuing vacuum, a third Arab-Israeli war erupted on June 5, 1967. At the conclusion of the short-lived Six Day War, Israel held not only its own territory but also the Gaza Strip, taken from Egypt; the Golan Heights, captured from Syria; and the West Bank of the Jordan River and east Jerusalem, both seized from Jordan. Nasserism was finished. With its demise, the Arabs entered a dark tunnel of self-doubt from which they have never emerged.

While the Israelis celebrated their stunning victory as confirmation of their ability to survive at the core of the Arab world, the 1967 war imposed humiliation on the Arabs. More than anything else, the Israeli conquest of Jerusalem drove home the reality that Israel was stronger than any combination of Arab states. This exposition of the weakness of the Arabs' military and political capabilities changed the relationship of the Arab states with each other and with the outside world. In the grim specter of more Palestinian refugees and more Palestinians under Israeli rule, the victims of 1948 saw the futility of placing their plight in the hands of the Arab states.

IN A SENSE, THE PALESTINIANS were the first to emerge from the dust of the disaster. They were led by a civil engineer named Yasir Arafat, who called the Palestinians to their own specific identity advanced by an organization known as the Palestine Liberation Organization (PLO). He was not alone in rousing the Palestinians to their own cause. Other leaders, of smaller groups, promoted a Marxist analysis of society rather than Arafat's ideology, which was no more complex than Palestinian nationalism. To the Marxists, the recovery of Palestine could be achieved only through a fundamental revolution in Arab society that would break the bonds of traditionalism.

For the Arabs who were not Palestinians, the events of 1967 sank deeply into their spirit and intensified the feeling that they lived in a world gone wrong. What followed was a period of anguished reappraisal of Arab culture and politics. The heroic age of the struggle for independence was over. No longer could the failures and deficiencies of Arab society be blamed on the power and intervention of the foreigner. Nor could the banalities of the old custodians of government in the 1920s and 1930s and the bravado of the post-World War II generation hide the realities of the Arab condition. In the harsh light of defeat, a younger generation began to ask difficult questions in societies not accustomed to self-appraisal and criticism. Disillusioned by pan-Arabism, they rendered a harsh verdict on the world erected first by the post-World War II nationalists and then by Gamal Abdel Nasser.

In the years immediately following 1967, the political scene in the Arab world changed and it stayed the same. Nasser died suddenly in 1970, leaving the seemingly inept Anwar Sadat as his successor. Hafiz al-Assad took command of Syria in a military coup the same year. One branch of the Arab-nationalist Baath Party, including the shadowy Saddam Hussein, had taken over Iraq in 1968. But in Jordan King Hussein continued to rule as did the dynasties of the Gulf states. In this political configuration, the Arabs across the Middle East were still licking the wounds of 1967 and searching for a new ideology to address the Arab condition when another seminal event shook the world of the Arabs.

In October 1973 Arab hopes of a renaissance once more soared in a unique convergence of politics and economics. Anwar Sadat of Egypt launched a new Arab war against Israel, and King Faisal of Saudi Arabia acquiesced to the move by the Organization of Petroleum Exporting Countries (OPEC) to almost quadruple oil prices in a petroleum market that had been tightening since the 1960s. At the same time, Saudi Arabia embargoed oil to the United States and the Netherlands, the major supporters of Israel. The sheer drama of spiraling oil prices, panicking consumers, and cascading wealth bestowed on the Arabs a power never known before. In perception, the predatory imperialists of the unconquerable West had been brought to their knees. Humbled, they would be made to pay for the psychological, political, and cultural dislocations they had inflicted on the Arab world. Thus, on the emotional level, the Arabs from the Persian Gulf across the Arab heartland were reborn.

Although Iraq possessed the second largest oil resources of the Persian Gulf and the sheikhdoms along the eastern coast of the Arabian Peninsula held major pieces of the oil market, it was Saudi Arabia that was most transformed by the oil boom. The insular, xenophobic Saudis were literally jerked out of centuries of isolation and thrust into a position of influence in Arab affairs and the world economy. Before they could accommodate to the new order, the Saudis, as well as other Arabs, came face-to-face with the reality that vast wealth derived from oil could generate weakness as well as strength.

In the realm of Arab unity, the explosion of petroleum prices in 1973–74 further opened the gaping chasm between the Arab world's rich and poor. In 1974 dollars, per capita income in Saudi Arabia was the equivalent of $6,991. It was $428 in Jordan, $340 in Syria, and a bare $240 in Egypt. Unwilling to share their wealth beyond providing jobs for migrants and doling out various forms of aid, the Saudis and others of the oil states lived as the rich in a neighborhood of paupers.

Yet within the oil states unimagined new riches brewed bitter new social tensions. Although their governments provided housing, health care, education, and social insurance through lavish public funding, the oil boom failed to achieve and sustain a high standard of living for all members of society. The reasons were the inequitable distribution of national income, restricted access to political power, and even faster population growth. The real beneficiaries of economic growth proved to be high-ranking government officials; army officers; those in command of technology; and businessmen engaged in construction or the import and export trade, or those connected to multinational enterprises. In essence, the pattern of the 1920s, 1930s, and 1940s that separated the Westernizing upper classes from the tradition-bound lower classes of the Fertile Crescent repeated itself on the Arabian Peninsula in the 1970s.

In the old society of the peninsula, inequalities of wealth in what were universally poor countries had been restrained by the social bonds and obligations of the tribe. After 1973 the pressures of modernization came so fast and so strong that not only were those social bonds weakened, but the inequalities between the haves and have-nots were clearly visible to the lower classes through the universality of the modern media. Moreover, every social class, regardless of position on the economic scale, felt the ramifications of the cataclysmic shift that came with the oil boom. The changing role of women altered the age-old family structure that had for centuries provided the individual his or her ultimate source of protection. Cultural influences delivered from abroad by foreign workers and foreign commerce breached the hallowed walls of tradition. The rapid expansion of education meant that children were being molded by their school as well as by their family. As a result, many sons and daughters were no longer willing to docilely assume their assigned place within the extended family. And those who pursued education abroad returned home with a whole range of new attitudes that caused them to question their elders both within the family and in the broader society.

Over the course of the 1970s the excess of demand for oil over supply narrowed. Consequently the bargaining position of OPEC grew weaker and prices fell. In the new economic conditions, the Arab sense of power over the West dissipated as oil producers came to understand that their markets—as well as their sources of capital goods, technical expertise, and advanced armaments with which to defend the oil resources—were largely in the West. Nor did oil alone give the Arabs the ability to dilute the West's support for Israel.

Despite the economic sledgehammer the Arabs picked up in 1973, the Palestinians in the regions occupied by Israel in the 1967 war remained a subject people in possession of diminishing amounts of land. The reasons lay in the Palestinian refusal to recognize the existence of Israel within its pre-1967 borders and the internal politics of Israel.

After the Six Day War, the key to peace between Israel and the Arabs rested in United Nations Resolutions 242 and 338. Saying essentially the same thing, both resolutions called on Israel to swap the West Bank, Gaza

Strip, and Golan Heights for recognition of the existence of the Israeli state and pledges of its security from the Arabs. But Arab governments refused to make peace with Israel in the absence of agreement by the Palestinians. In 1977 a flurry of diplomatic activity directed by Washington attempted to achieve resolution of the conflict between Israel and the Arabs that had plagued the Middle East since 1948. In the end it failed, in large part because Yasir Arafat could not or would not deliver the PLO to the negotiating table. As a consequence, Egypt's Anwar Sadat made his historic trip to Jerusalem to pursue a separate peace with Israel. It came at a time of profound political change in Israel.

Israel's Labor Party, dominated by Western Europeans who hewed to the socialist ideology of the original Zionists, had always regarded the occupied territories as bargaining chips to win recognition and security from Israel's Arab neighbors. During the 1970s Labor's hold on government, which had been unbroken since the founding of the state, began to be challenged by the nationalistic, antisocialist ideology of the Likud Party. In 1977 the Likud, strengthened by large numbers of newly arrived Russian Jews who wanted nothing to do with the economics of the socialism they had just escaped, broke Labor's hold on government and with it Israeli policy based on the formula of land for peace.

Although the Labor government had placed settlements of Jews in the occupied territories soon after the war of 1967, the reasons were largely strategic. For the ultranationalist Likud government of Polish-born Menachem Begin (former commander of the underground paramilitary Irgun Zvai Leumi), the raison d'être of settlements, particularly those on the West Bank, was the incorporation into Israel of what Jewish ultranationalists called Samaria and Judea. Begin and the extremist Zionist organization's clash with David Ben-Gurion and the more moderate Zionist armed forces during the 1948 war for Palestine set up the basic dynamic of Israeli politics. Thus, as the Likud aggressively built new Jewish settlements on land expropriated from Palestinians, the formula for peace devised in 1967 became more complicated.

Although Yasir Arafat, speaking for the Palestine Liberation Organization, denounced what Palestinians saw as colonization, neither the leader nor his group could alter the situation on the ground. Neither could the Arab states. Military action against Israel was impossible given the superior armed might of the Israeli state, backed by the United States. Furthermore, the competing interests of the Arab governments guaranteed that Arab unity remained what it had long been—mythology. Even though a political union between two or more Arab states was still discussed, the civil war in Lebanon that began in 1975 and the Egyptian peace with Israel that came in the 1979 Camp David Accords was the reality. The Arab world was splintered and impotent. Every Arab felt in some degree that all the promises of independence were dead, the dreams of Arab nationalism had vanished, the promises of social reform under the rubric of "Arab socialism" had evaporated. All that was left were the recriminations, doubts, and anxieties of 1967.

IN JANUARY 1979 THE VORTEX OF MIDDLE EAST events shifted eastward when the issues of identity and social justice, wrapped in the ideology of politicized Islam, swept Muhammad Reza Shah off the throne of Iran. It was a revolution that came out of Islam's dissenting Shiite sect, which rose out of Persian culture as opposed to Arab culture. Yet in the Arab world, Islam as politics resonated among the masses crammed in crowded cities who were hungering for an idealized past amid the tumult and deprivations of the present. No Arab leader felt the threat of religious revolution more than Saddam Hussein, the president of Iraq, who seized total power in July 1979 and ruled a population in which 60 percent shared Shiite Islam with Ayatollah Ruhollah Khomeini.

Under verbal assault from Tehran, which he perceived as threatening his political life, Saddam Hussein in September 1980 sent Iraq's army into Iran to stop the advance of the Islamic revolution at the eastern front of the Arab world. Over the next eight years the oil-rich monarchies of the Arabian Peninsula, motivated by their own fears of revolutionary Islam, would finance the Iraqi-Iranian bloodbath along the Shatt al-Arab, the waterway dividing Iraq and Iran.

On the western side of the Arab world, civil war had been raging in Lebanon since 1975. Although the conflict was seen in the West as a religious war between Christians and Muslims, the essential question that pitted Lebanese against Lebanese was one of identity. That question asked whether Lebanon was a part of the Western world, as many Christians claimed, or whether it belonged to the Arab world as a consequence of Arab culture and language. While the Muslims almost universally saw themselves as part of the Arab world, the Christians divided on what was both a political and existential issue of identity for themselves and their country. But the Lebanese were not left alone to define themselves.

In June 1982 the war suddenly ratcheted up when Israel, intent on destroying the political and military infrastructure that the PLO had erected in Lebanon over the past dozen years, sent its well-armed and disciplined army over the border of its northern neighbor. Through much of the summer Israeli air power pounded Beirut, eventually forcing Yasir Arafat and the political/military structure of the PLO to accept an American-brokered withdrawal to Tunis. They left behind the largely young, old, and female Palestinians of Beirut. Two weeks later somewhere between 800 and 2,000 of those Palestinians living in the camps of Sabra and Shatilla were massacred by the Phalange, Israel's far-right Christian allies, who hated the Palestinians for having created a mini-state in Lebanon. In far-off Tunis, the PLO could do nothing but add the victims' names to the ranks of martyrs to the Palestinian cause.

Deprived of both PLO and Arab leadership, Palestinians in the West Bank and Gaza in December 1987 picked up stones and hurled them at the Israeli army of occupation. It was the beginning of the intifada, an Arabic word meaning "shaking off." The uprising not only challenged Israel from inside the occupied territories but also altered the relationship of Palestinians with each other. Using their own blood, the rebels drew a line between those who lived in Israeli-occupied territories and those who lived outside; and between themselves and other Arabs who had claimed since 1948 to carry the torch of Palestinian grievances. Defiance by young men burning tires and old women throwing rocks gave the Palestinians a sense of power they had never felt before. Unable to put down what was a popular uprising with little organization or leadership, the Israeli government found itself on the defensive against both foreign criticism of excessive force and an Israeli public deeply divided over how to respond to Palestinian rage. But neither the Arabs nor the Palestinians seized the moment to act as one.

King Hussein of Jordan, the self-appointed guardian of the Palestinians, surrendered his claim because few were any longer willing to follow. Egypt stood by its peace treaty with Israel. The other Arab states provided little but rhetoric. Although the PLO from Tunis attempted to exert leadership over the intifada, it was the Palestinians on the ground who carried the battle to Israel. That opened the question of who among the Palestinians held the right to lead the struggle for a Palestinian state and who possessed the legitimate authority to govern it—the Palestinians of the diaspora or those living in the occupied territories. Yet the greatest blow to unity among the Arabs came when Saddam Hussein of Arab Iraq invaded Arab Kuwait.

When the Iraqi army rolled into Kuwait at 2 a.m. on August 2, 1990, the Arab world convulsed. Hallowed dogmas, sanctified identity, and celebrated unity, all cultivated and defended since the last days of the Ottoman Empire, dissolved under the blasphemy of Saddam Hussein. Left without their bearings, the Arabs reacted differently to the affront of Baghdad. From the core of the Arab world, Egypt, Syria, Saudi Arabia, and war-battered Lebanon took their position against Iraq. Jordan, Yemen, and the PLO stood, if somewhat reluctantly, with Saddam Hussein. When the American-led Gulf War came in January 1991, Saddam Hussein suffered a humiliating defeat. Saved from political annihilation by the decision of a 30-nation alliance to stop the war short of Baghdad, Saddam Hussein refused to surrender.

For more than a decade he has sacrificed his own people to the economic sanctions imposed by the United Nations Security Council in order to protect his weapons of mass destruction. In his refusal to bow before American pressure, which has kept the sanctions in place, he has stirred some of the deepest emotions of the Arabs, who for decades have felt that Arab pride and dignity have been trampled under the arrogance and power of the West. The brashness with which Saddam Hussein has confronted the United States, the patron and protector of Israel, has given the Arab on the street a new hero after almost two decades in which no heroic figure has attempted to banish Arab frustrations and disappointments. Still, Saddam Hussein has not been able to reverse the downward economic spiral of most Arabs. Nor has the most repressive tyrant of the region been able to deliver the Arab renaissance. And he has not bestowed on the Palestinians their state in the occupied territories, something they came to expect from

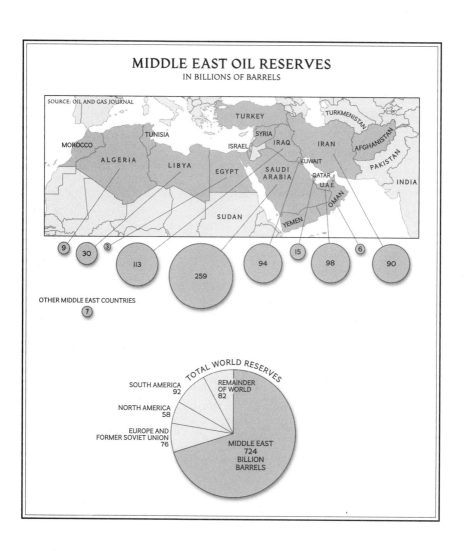

MIDDLE EAST OIL RESERVES
IN BILLIONS OF BARRELS

SOURCE: OIL AND GAS JOURNAL

TURKEY
TURKMENISTAN
TUNISIA
SYRIA
MOROCCO
ISRAEL
IRAQ
IRAN
AFGHANISTAN
ALGERIA
LIBYA
KUWAIT
PAKISTAN
EGYPT
SAUDI ARABIA
QATAR
INDIA
U.A.E.
OMAN
SUDAN
YEMEN

9
30
3
113
259
94
15
98
6
90

OTHER MIDDLE EAST COUNTRIES
7

TOTAL WORLD RESERVES

SOUTH AMERICA
92

REMAINDER OF WORLD
82

NORTH AMERICA
58

EUROPE AND FORMER SOVIET UNION
76

MIDDLE EAST
724
BILLION
BARRELS

the conditions set in the Oslo Accords of 1993, which drew the road map for Israeli-Palestinian accommodation.

AT THE TURN OF THE MILLENNIUM any observer of the Arab countries saw societies in conflict. The ties of culture strengthened in the 20th century by mass communication and easy movement across national boundaries had proved insufficient to produce the political unity that the ideology of Arab nationalism had so long touted. Increasing wealth, unevenly distributed between states and within states, called the masses to question the justice of the social order and the legitimacy of their governments. Yet these same regimes not only had been in power over several decades but appeared to be in no immediate danger of collapse.

This specter of enduring regimes governing deeply disturbed societies may have appeared to be a paradox. But it reflected real politics. The regimes of Egypt, Saudi Arabia, Jordan, Syria, and Iraq claimed a degree of stability because in each a cohesive ruling group had successfully linked its interests with those of other powerful elements in society. Ideologically, this alliance of interests was expressed in various countries in various forms, ranging from state-operated welfare, to intractable opposition to Israel, to guardianship of the holiest cities of Islam. It was enough to create the illusion that the rulers were reasonably legitimate in the eyes of society, or at least a significant part of it. There were tangible reasons why. First, these governments, unlike those of the early 20th century, possessed means of control in the form of armies and security services that enabled them to inject their authority into every village and almost every house. Second, these regimes, in performance of the legitimate tasks of modern government, provided education, health care, public utilities, and a range of economic services and benefits somewhat commensurate with the resources of the particular country. Consequently, a vast percentage of the population became tied into or, more important, dependent in numerous ways on the government in power. Concerned with their own personal welfare, a majority of people were willing, at least up to a point, to help maintain the regime in power.

Still there existed, as it has existed since the late 19th century, a deep and troubling sense among most Arabs that Arab society suffers from a lack of direction, mission, and accomplishment. Once, most of those who sought release from their discontent looked to Arab nationalism. Until the collapse of the Soviet Union stripped its ideology bare, Marxism promised redemption to others. Today many see the answer to the malaise of the Arab world in Islam. For it is there that they find a mystical, utopian alternative to the wretched reality in which so many in the Arab world live.

Islam as a political ideology is not new. There has always existed among Arab Muslims a sense of common destiny for those who have inherited the religion of Islam. This attitude is shared by Arab Christians in the context of a shared language as opposed to religion. In the 20th century, Islam as politics became more defined. In Egypt in 1929, a group known as the Muslim Brotherhood organized around the tenet that modern society, like traditional society, could be structured only on the doctrines and laws of Islam. It was an idea that drew followers among the urban populations, where the poor laborers and the not-so-poor craftsmen and small tradesmen, as well as professionals shut out of the charmed circle of the dominant elite, responded to the Brothers' Islamic political ideology.

During the 1940s and 1950s, some within the elites who led the nationalist movements also drew on words and images associated with Islam to define a collective Arab future. But the Islam of the modernizers was not the Islam of the Muslim Brotherhood. Nor was its aim theocratic government. Rather the modernizers sought to reformulate the faith in order to enable society to meet the challenges of modernization.

Even through the years in which Nasser strode across the landscape of the Arab world waving the banner of secular Arab nationalism, a certain Islamic element remained important in that combination of ideas that made up the political thought of the era. When the crushing defeat of the Six Day War came, it led many Arabs to ask whether societal redemption might be found in the religious/cultural tradition that had once given order and meaning to Arab life.

The oil boom of the 1970s only intensified the ideological contest between the present and the past. The Syrian philosopher Sadiq Jalal al-Azm declared that religious thought was not only false, it was dangerous. In supporting the existing order of society and those who controlled it,

Islam stood in the way of genuine social and political liberation. Few other writers went this far. Most discussed Islam as a body of religious belief encased in a body of inherited culture. To them, what the Arabs needed was a genuine historical understanding of the Islamic past, coupled with a willingness to transcend that past by selecting elements of Islamic culture, language, and tradition, to mold a new future. Finally, there were the Islamists who held that Islam was more than a culture. For them, Islam was not only a faith, it was also politics and economics.

By the end of the 1970s, Islam within the Arab political model seemed to slide backward from reform to tradition as the less educated wrenched the question of faith and politics from the intellectuals. They, in turn, moved Islam as politics from discourse to action. This new Islamic militancy was fueled by the example of the Islamic revolution in Iran, which, in the Arab world, played against the background of bulging cities constantly fed by rural immigrants escaping the overpopulated countryside.

Finding jobs as manual laborers, watchmen, or peddlers, the new arrivals, even more than their predecessors, lived in a society in which they were largely observers and victims rather than participants and beneficiaries. Like those in the mass migrations of the 1950s and the 1960s, these refugees from rural poverty became urbanized to a degree. But the cities to which they came also became ruralized. Cut off from the ties of kinship and neighbors that held the society of the villages together, the rural refugees counterbalanced their deep sense of alienation from the political and economic system with the assurance that they belonged to a universal community of Islam. Within that community, there were values and rules expressed in a language that they not only understood but one in which they could express their own grievances and aspirations. Those who wished to mobilize these urban masses for political action had to use the same language. Thus Islam became a force of opposition to Western power; to those accused of being subservient to Western influence; to governments regarded as corrupt, ineffective, and immoral; and to societies that seemed to have lost their meaning and direction.

Despite repression by some regimes and bribery by others, politicized Islam sent its power against those branded "oppressor." In November 1979 Islamic militants seized the Grand Mosque of Mecca in a dramatic statement of opposition to the House of Saud. The Muslim Brotherhood assassinated Egyptian president Anwar Sadat in 1981 and attempted to topple Syria's Hafiz Al-Assad in 1982. In 1984 Hezbollah, militants from within the Shiite sect, delivered bombs by truck to a military barracks and the American Embassy in Lebanon, forcing the U.S. military presence out of the country. In later years they snatched Americans off the streets of Beirut to become hostages of their clandestine power.

Through the 1990s and into the new century, Islam as politics marched on. In the absence of an agreement with Israel on a Palestinian state, Hamas, Islamic Jihad, and other Islamic groups among the Palestinians drained power away from Yasir Arafat and the PLO. Elsewhere, imams in the mosques of Egypt preached religious revolution. And in Saudi Arabia the House of Saud, built on the foundations of the ultraconservative Wahhabi sect of Islam, faced the ideology of Osama bin Laden. Scion of one of the kingdom's leading families, he held the royal family responsible for the corruption of the faith that underpinned its legitimacy. From his base in Afghanistan, he indoctrinated and trained his own army of terror.

On September 11, 2001, the stealth power of militant Islam struck New York's World Trade Center as well as the Pentagon in Washington. The perpetrators and those who supported them had sent their message of anger against Western cultural intrusion, continued Israeli dominance of the Palestinians, repressive governments undergirded by American support, and the failings of their own societies. In the most inhuman of acts, carried out under the most contorted ideology, the merciless hijackers of four airliners demanded change in their world.

IF RADICAL POLITICAL CHANGE DOES SWEEP across all or part of the Arab world, it may come in the name of an Islamic ideal of justice. But just what that ideal is and how to achieve it encompasses a spectrum of views. For the true believers, every aspect of life is wrapped in Islam. To them, the government belongs to the *ulama*, the learned clerics of Islam, who as men of peace or men of jihad direct their followers. For others, the Islamic ideal means a society derived from the cumulative tradition of Islam, carefully and reasonably applied to the conditions of today. In this Islamic system the clerics would not rule, for tradition holds that they should remain separate from government, and skepticism warns that religious leaders are as susceptible to the corruption of power and wealth as secular rulers.

But the Islamic view, however it is expressed, is only one side of the intense debate among Arabs on the nature of society and governance. The other side is largely populated by a generation that has grown up since the oil boom, many of whom have been educated in Western schools and universities. In their perception, the enemy is no longer colonialism, Israel, or dominance by the West. Rather it is the cancerous growth of Islamic extremism operating on the fringes of the political system. Fueled by dogmatic clerics and legions of the poorly educated, Islamic militancy threatens their realization of political and economic power more than the regimes currently ruling them.

Nevertheless, the middle class—no more than the lower classes—cannot escape the wrenching social, economic, political, and psychological problems in which the Arabs have been entangled since 1920. The questions to which they seek answers are the same questions that have arisen, faded, and arisen again through the 20th century and into the 21st. How can Arabs define their identity? How can the malaise of Arab society be ended? How can the issues of poverty, human rights, and corrupt political systems be addressed? How can the yoke of Israel that has for so long added its weight to the problems of the Arab world be lifted? And how can the West be made to understand that democracy, which took hundreds of years to develop in the West, cannot be achieved overnight in the Middle East?

The Arabs are not alone in their search for definition. Non-Arab societies in the broadly defined Middle East are also engaged in a similar, if not as profound or multifaceted, search for definition. The irony is that these are the old societies of Turkey and Iran, which are grounded in long histories and strong identities. At the end of the Ottoman Empire, Turkey deliberately chose the path of secularism and modernization under the guidance of Kemal Atatürk. Although the intervening hand of the military has held Turkey to its secular system and to the concept of democracy, the political system has never escaped from the tensions created by Islamic traditionalism. The reason is that there are two Turkeys of unequal size and potency. The larger and stronger looks west and to the future, the smaller looks east and to the past.

In Iran a theocracy emerged from the revolution of 1979, which was waged against a corrupt, repressive monarchy in the name of social justice. From within this theocracy two decades later, the Iranians have found that a government based on Islam does not necessarily end corruption or produce social justice. They have also learned that clerics who may be able to preach cannot always govern. Trapped in a revolution in which the orthodoxy of Ayatollah Khomeini and the self-interests of his disciples will not allow evolution, the Iranians have realized that although Islam can provide the moral glue for society, it is not the panacea for all ills arising from the challenges of modernization.

Even the Israelis, who had such a clear vision of themselves in 1948 and 1967, have not escaped the essential question of identity for themselves or the definition of their state. Today the Israelis are almost equally split between those who see Israel as a secular state built on Jewish culture and those who see it as some form of a theocracy ruling over the restored Kingdom of David. Like the Arab states, Israel, in its own unique way, is also a transitional society. The great ingathering of the Jews of the many diasporas has created a country that is indisputably Jewish, populated by people with recent roots in Western Europe, Eastern Europe, Russia, the United States, Morocco, Iraq, Yemen, Ethiopia, and anywhere else from which an immigrant has come. Within the borders of Israel, Jewish nationalism is the ideal that jostles with the cultural traditions of places as widely dispersed as the Jews themselves. And while the Israelis endeavor to find physical security amid another Palestinian uprising, this one waged through acts of terrorism, they also struggle with each other over the essence of the Israeli state and its territorial boundaries.

In the early years of the 21st century the Middle East, lying at the crossroads between Asia and Europe, is a region of unfulfilled aspirations, overwhelming problems, and the bitterest of rivalries. It is also a region of high culture—Arab, Jewish, Iranian, and Turkish—and a region of critical importance for most of the world.

Crossing the worn stones of Jerusalem, an Orthodox Jew hurries toward one of the gates to the Old City. Jerusalem has been at the heart of Judaism since the tenth century B.C., when Solomon built the Temple there to house the Ark of the Covenant.

CHAPTER SIX

JUDAISM

HEAR, O ISRAEL

YOSSI KLEIN HALEVI

JUDAISM IS THE LOVE STORY BETWEEN GOD AND THE JEWISH
people. Invariably tempestuous, in turn unrequited and exalted, that
romance forms the basis for 3,000 years of evolving religious observance
and national identity. According to the Hebrew Bible, God at times
accuses the Jews of faithlessness to his commandments and punishes them
with exile from the land of Israel. For their part, Jews sometimes recip-
rocate by accusing God of abandoning his covenant with Israel and turn
away from him in anger, as many have done in the aftermath of the
Holocaust. But so long as the Jewish people exist, the love story persists.

Though Judaism has directly spawned one universalist religion,
Christianity, and profoundly influenced another, Islam, it remains a specific faith for a specific people. Unlike Christianity and Islam, it doesn't
aspire to convert the world, only to Judaize the Jewish people. Judaism
believes that it is the only path to God for Jews; non-Jews who lead
moral lives don't need to become Jews in order to reach heaven. Though
Judaism is confined to one people—Jews—they aren't defined by blood

or race. Conversion has always been part of Judaism, and the Jewish people are represented by nearly every ethnicity, which a stroll through downtown Jerusalem today immediately reveals. The combination of peoplehood and faith creates ongoing tension among Jews over Jewish identity. According to Jewish law, anyone born a Jew remains part of the Jewish people, even if he or she no longer practices Judaism or believes in God or even converts to another religion. Yet the only way a non-Jew can join the Jewish people is by converting to the Jewish faith.

Judaism, which introduced monotheism to humanity, has uncompromising beliefs about reality. As a legal and moral system, it offers a clearly defined way of life. Yet most Jews relate to Judaism first of all as the story of a people. The Hebrew Bible is at once the basis of religious law and the historical epic of the Jewish people in their formative years. The Jewish holidays—from Passover, which celebrates the exodus from Egypt toward the Promised Land, to the fast of Tisha b'Ab, which mourns the exile of the Jewish people from the Promised Land—recount moments of the Jewish encounter with God in history. When Ruth the Moabite converted to Judaism by telling her Israelite mother-in-law, Naomi, "Your people are my people, and your God is my God," she defined the progression of Jewish identity: first commitment to peoplehood, then commitment to faith.

The centrality of peoplehood in Judaism tends to obscure the religious definition of a "good Jew." While other faiths judge heretics on the basis of their rejection of religious dogma or ritual, Judaism's judgment is more ambivalent. The "evil son" of the Haggadah—the Passover text recounting the exodus from Egypt—is defined as one who refers to fellow Jews as "you" rather than "us." The contemporary Jewish philosopher Rabbi David Hartman notes that "the heretic in the tradition is one who does not feel solidarity and empathy with the joys and suffering of his community." Conversely, someone who violates the most basic religious practices but helps protect or enhance the Jewish people is considered a loyal if lax Jew. The question of who is a "good Jew" is hardly theoretical: In the heated cultural conflict between secular and ultra-Orthodox Israelis today, the ultra-Orthodox accuse secularists of betraying Judaism by assimilating into the hedonistic culture of the West. For their part, secularists fault ultra-Orthodox young men for choosing military deferments to further their religious studies and insist that they themselves are "better Jews," because they serve in the army and risk their lives to defend the Jewish state.

JEWS PASSIONATELY ARGUE OVER EVERY ASPECT of their tradition—from faith in a benevolent and all-powerful God, to faith in themselves as the chosen people. During 2,000 years of exile, Jews prayed for a return to the land of Israel, imagining that event as triggering the messianic revelation of God's presence on Earth. Yet, now that the return has happened, Jews can't decide whether the state of Israel should be invested with religious meaning or treated simply as a secular entity. An ancient Jewish saying notes that the Bible has "70 faces," or multiple interpretations, and Judaism, more than ever before, is defined by its contradictory interpretations of Jewish history and faith. A West Bank settler and an Israeli peace activist; an ultra-Orthodox Jew who opposes any change in the tradition and a Reform rabbi who officiates at weddings of intermarried couples—all claim to represent the authentic spirit of Judaism. Jews can't even agree anymore over how to define membership in the Jewish people. Orthodox Jews insist on the traditional definition of a Jew as someone born to a Jewish mother (or who is converted to Judaism under Orthodox auspices), while Reform Jews insist that anyone born to a Jewish father or mother should be considered a Jew. The state of Israel goes further: Under its "Law of Return," anyone with a single Jewish grandparent is eligible for repatriation to the Jewish homeland and automatic Israeli citizenship, though the state's criterion for Israeli citizenship doesn't presume to offer a religious definition for who is a Jew.

Jewish survival, however essential and celebrated, isn't perceived by Judaism as an end in itself. Instead, the goal of Judaism, as it evolved through the biblical era, became the redemption of humanity, the imposition of universal justice and God's revelation on Earth. By introducing the notion of a messianic endpoint to history, Judaism challenged the ancient world's prevailing notion of cyclical time with its own vision of linear time— that is, of the human experience as story. The Jewish understanding of that story is embodied in the biblical narrative, which begins with the creation of the world and its high point, the creation of humanity;

moves to the creation of the Jewish people as the carrier of the message of monotheism and the hope of redemption; and culminates in the prophetic visions of the messianic era. Jews explain the fact that the Bible begins with the story of creation and the Garden of Eden (rather than with Abraham and the birth of the Jewish people) as a reminder that the very purpose of Jewish existence is the messianic restoration of humanity to the Garden—that state of being where all of life is perceived as an interconnected whole. Jews end every prayer service by invoking the messianic era, when humanity will acknowledge God as sovereign: "In that day God will be one and His name one." The unification of humanity— not through mass conversion to Judaism but to monotheism—is the goal of Jewish existence.

Judaism posits a divine paradoxical strategy for achieving that oneness: setting aside a people as an experiment for, and the agent of, redemption. It is precisely the attempt to elevate a people—rather than an elect group of saints—through an almost unbearable intimacy with God that transforms Jewish history into a test case for the intimacy of God with all peoples. Jewish peoplehood, then, is central to Judaism because it is central to Judaism's mission of redemption.

Once a week, on the Sabbath, Jews are meant to experience a foretaste of a perfected world. An equalizing day of rest from labor to which every Jew is obliged, the Sabbath is arguably the most revolutionary idea introduced by Judaism into the ancient world. As a reprieve from the pressures and routines of the week, the Sabbath, which begins at sundown on Friday and ends at sundown on Saturday, simulates an experience of timelessness. The paradox of the Sabbath is liberation through restriction. The observant Jew refrains from travel and commerce and the use of electrical appliances and, in that suspension of relentless modernity, he becomes archaic, freed from time. The Sabbath is the most beloved of all Jewish observances, widely considered by Jews to be Judaism's greatest gift, an intimation of redemption in an unredeemed world. Hardly an ascetic experience, the Sabbath is a time of delight, when the best meals of the week are served and marital relations encouraged. More than the Jews preserving the Sabbath, the Zionist philosopher Ahad Ha'am wrote, the Sabbath has preserved the Jews.

Along with the Sabbath, one other central element of Judaism has sustained the Jewish people with its promise of redemption: the return to the land of Israel. Even in periods when the Jews weren't in possession of the land, its memory remained central to Jewish consciousness, especially during prayer, for which return to Zion is a major theme. Jews perceived exile as an aberration, a prison sentence the Jewish people needed to serve for having been spiritually unworthy of living in the Holy Land. "Bitter like the exile," went a Yiddish saying, invoked to express a painful experience. The Bible promised that God would one day return the Jews from dispersion and that hope offered a culmination to the seemingly endless exile.

Other religions cherish the Holy Land and the Holy City; but only Judaism has tied its origins, its destiny, and its very existence to the land of Israel and to Jerusalem. There are no Jewish people and no Judaism without the land of Israel. A religious Jew invokes Zion and Jerusalem dozens of times a day in daily prayers and blessings: "Return to Your city Jerusalem with mercy," "Gather us together from the four corners of the earth to our land." Commitment to the land of Israel accompanies a Jew at decisive moments of the life cycle. A groom breaks a glass under the wedding canopy to evoke mourning over the destruction of the Jerusalem Temple, a shattering in the wholeness of the universe. Some Jews who live in the Diaspora arrange to be buried in the land of Israel. Love for the land is more than national or historic sentiment but central to Judaism's messianic strategy. Judaism needs a land in which to conduct its controlled experiment for the redemption of humanity. A holy people anchored in a holy land is a promise for the ultimate holiness of all peoples and all lands.

THE FOCAL POINT OF JEWISH MESSIANIC LONGING was almost always national—the ingathering of the exiles into the land of Israel, the restoration of Jewish sovereignty there, and the rebuilding of the Jerusalem Temple. The fulfillment of that vision would then lead to an era of world peace. The closest that Judaism has produced to a normative messianic theology was formulated by Maimonides, a 12th-century North African rabbi, philosopher, physician, and legal codifier and one of Judaism's most influential thinkers. Maimonides envisioned the messianic era unfolding through natural rather than miraculous means (with the notable exception of the resurrection of the dead). According to Maimonides, then, the messiah will be recognizable not by supernatural signs but by his ability to end the domination of the nations over the Jewish people and bring world peace. The messiah will be a mortal king, whose progeny will continue to rule Israel. The dynasty's goal will be the creation of a just and stable order in which the contemplative life is preeminent.

For all its messianic hopes, and the periodic appearance in Jewish history of messianic pretenders, Judaism has, for the most part, avoided utopian temptations and apocalyptic hysteria and remained a stubbornly practical faith. If you are planting a field and you hear that the messiah has arrived, cautioned the first-century rabbi Yohanan Ben Zakkai, continue planting. Jewish thinkers have consistently affirmed the primacy of small nurturing acts of daily life over the vast and hidden processes of the divine plan in history. Indeed, history is redeemed not through great upheaval but through the accumulated small acts of good performed by individuals throughout the generations, which ultimately tip the balance against evil and allow redemption to emerge, seemingly from nowhere.

Judaism expresses that commitment to incremental holiness through its system of mitzvoth, divine commandments. Mitzvoth are acts of sanctification, Judaism's strategy for the gradual transformation of the mundane into the sacred. Judaism views the material world as potentially holy. Physicality isn't denied but directed and elevated, refined by human intervention. On the individual level, mitzvoth enable a Jew to transform daily life into divine service, inserting an awareness of God's presence into the most commonplace acts. A Jew can recite literally a hundred blessings a day, waking up with the prayer thanking God for preserving his soul in his body and retiring to bed with the sh'ma, the prayer of God's oneness. By blessing and by placing limitations on physical acts, Judaism seeks to transform instinct into intention. Blessing one's food transforms the dining table into an altar; refraining from intercourse during menstruation and then immersing in a ritual bath before lovemaking turns the body into an instrument for holiness and relationship into a sacred ritual. Judaism, then, is a process— slow and infinitely patient—of human transformation. It is optimistic about human nature, but cautiously realistic, accepting imperfection as a given, even as it aspires to the eventual perfection of humanity.

Jewish tradition has identified 613 mitzvoth in the Bible. Those mitzvoth form the basis for the many thousands of rabbinic interpretive rulings through the centuries on issues ranging from matters of life and death to the most mundane aspects of daily routine, collectively called halakah, "the way," a word that implies active movement, process. At its best, halakah is a system that not only imposes rules but also addresses the practical and spiritual needs of its adherents, the process whereby God's commandments are interpreted by human beings and integrated into human reality. While Orthodox Jews aspire to fulfill all the commandments (other than those connected to Temple worship, which are no longer relevant), most Jews today observe "mitzvoth" rather than "the mitzvoth." That is, they honor those commandments that conform to their own understanding of Jewish identity and commitment.

The struggle within halakah—among the rabbis entrusted by the Jewish people through the centuries with the process of interpreting Jewish law—has always been over determining how much change the system can bear. halakah seeks to mediate between strict legal interpretation and human and spiritual needs, and each generation of rabbis reevaluates the balance between those two poles.

Mitzvoth are divided into various categories. There are mitzvoth, like leaving the land fallow on the sabbatical year, that can be performed only in the land of Israel, and mitzvoth, like observing the Sabbath, that aren't bound by geography. There are mitzvoth, like the commandment to love your neighbor, meant to enhance the relationship between human beings; mitzvot, like charity, with a clear moral imperative; and those, like the prohibition against wearing clothes made of wool and linen, whose purpose remains a divine mystery. Some Jews explain the intricate laws of keeping kosher on a moral basis: By forbidding a Jew to eat meat and dairy products together, for example, Judaism insists on an awareness that taking an animal's life is more serious than eating its by-products. And by forbidding certain foods, Judaism places a limit on human appetite and sanctifies the act of eating.

Judaism emphasizes the performance of mitzvoth far more than it does faith. Not that faith is irrelevant: Throughout history Jews have willingly been martyred for their faith in the God of Israel. But Judaism insists that faith emerges from deed. The seminal moment of Jewish commitment to action occurred at Mount Sinai: "We will do and we will listen," the children of Israel proclaimed when God offered them the Torah. That is: We'll fulfill the commandments even before we try to understand them—an affirmation of the Judaic belief that understanding results from experience.

Because of its emphasis on daily life and its preference for deeds over faith, along with its focus on repairing and ultimately redeeming the world, Judaism is often called a this-worldly religion. Still, Judaic teachings constantly recall that this world is but a "narrow bridge," a "corridor" to the world to come. Like all the great faiths, Judaism seeks to guide an individual's soul through this world for its return home. Judaism contains a vast— and fully normative—mystical tradition known as kabbalah (literally, "received tradition"), which aims to reveal the "concealed" aspects of Torah, transforming mitzvoth into the tool for intimacy with God and, more audaciously, for becoming God's partner in healing the world.

According to the 16th-century kabbalist Isaac Luria, who lived in the land of Israel and is perhaps the most influential Jewish mystic, a cosmic shattering occurred at the very moment of creation. In this cosmology, the divine light was too powerful for the "vessels" that contained it; the material world, with all its imperfections, was formed from those shattered vessels, which conceal the divine light. The existence of evil and imperfection, then, is a result of the rupture in creation. The task of a human being is to free the divine sparks lost and embedded in physicality, and the means for doing so are the mitzvoth, permeated by contemplative kabbalistic "intentions" that seek to unite this world with the spiritual worlds above.

Kabbalah's goal is twofold. On the collective level, it is a tool for redemption, for healing a wounded cosmos. And like all mystical traditions, it offers the individual a way to achieve intimacy with the divine. Kabbalah deals intensively with the various levels and qualities of the soul; much of Kabbalah accepts reincarnation as a given. And where Maimonides, as a rationalist, described immortality as the survival of the intellect, engaged in contemplation of God, the kabbalists wrote at length about the transmigration of souls between the worlds of body and spirit.

Through most of the period of exile, the mystical and the rational coexisted as parallel, legitimate approaches. By the late Middle Ages, kabbalah had come to be almost universally accepted as the deepest level of Jewish wisdom. Beginning in the 19th century, though, much of mainstream Judaism in the West turned increasingly rationalist, dismissing mysticism as a superstitious throwback. But the dual shocks of the Holocaust and the return to the land of Israel have reawakened longings for the experience of God's presence; and the kabbalah's vision of a shattered cosmos requiring spiritual healing has become compelling for many post-Holocaust Jews. As a result, the study and practice of mysticism are once again spreading through the Jewish world.

MYSTICS OR RATIONALISTS, BELIEVERS OR ATHEISTS, what unites all Jews is love for the Jewish story. Jews may vehemently disagree over the meaning and implications of their story, but all who define themselves as Jews believe that the saga of a people who have maintained an intimate dialogue with their most ancient memories under the most trying conditions is worth transmitting to their children. Each generation of Jews shares a sense of responsibility, even awe, at finding itself caretaker of the Jewish story, and Jews of every generation fear that the story may end with them. They feel an almost maternal protectiveness toward their collective existence, which seems at once indestructible and unbearably vulnerable. The unlikely persistence of the Jewish people through an often hostile historical terrain is widely seen by Jews as a miracle and is one of the most compelling proofs Jews cite for belief in God. In the eternity of the Jewish people, the Jew glimpses the Eternal. "The continued survival of the Jewish people," wrote Gershom Scholem, the late scholar of Jewish mysticism, "seems to suggest that the Jews have in fact been chosen by someone for something." In that tentative acknowledgment of Judaism's two basic premises— the existence of God and the chosenness of Israel—Scholem speaks for many Jews today, who aren't quite sure what the Jewish story means but who sense the transcendent in its very endurance. That belief has been reinforced by the rebirth of Jewish sovereignty in the land of Israel immediately following the Holocaust. In that almost instant and overwhelming shift from utter powerlessness to unprecedented power, many Jews sense not only the assertion of their national will but also of divine intervention, the reemergence of the biblical God of Israel who actively intervenes to protect his people.

The Jewish story begins with a summons: God dispatching Abraham from the land of his birth to "the land that I will show you." Implicit in the story of the man Jews affectionately call *Avraham Avinu,* Abraham our Father, are the essential themes of the Jewish story generally. First, there is the centrality of the Holy Land. The forerunner of the Jewish nation (who is believed to have lived around 1850 B.C.) is introduced through the act of settling the land of Israel. Then the Bible explains the purpose of Abraham's mission as redemptive: "In you shall all the families of the earth be blessed." Finally, God reveals that he has chosen Abraham to found a nation that will embody justice: "I have made myself known to him so that he should command his children and his household after him to keep the path of the Lord, to do loving-kindness and justice." Still, Jews don't perceive the Bible as a work of self-congratulation. Instead, they study it as a sobering account of the gap between vision and reality, of their often failed struggle to transcend human limitation and become a holy nation, as God commands.

The commitment to justice could even lead to questioning God's ways, as in Abraham's argument with God over the destruction of the cities of Sodom and Gomorrah. The legitimacy of struggle with the divine was confirmed with Abraham's grandson, Jacob, who was awarded the name "Israel" after wrestling with an angel. Jews interpret this to mean that the task of Israel is to "wrestle" with God, to avoid complacency, and to struggle with faith and meaning.

According to the Bible, the progeny of Jacob sought refuge in Egypt from famine in the land of Israel, were eventually enslaved, and finally were freed through a series of miracles—a divine plan to create a people who would empathize with the suffering of others, who would love the stranger, the widow, and the orphan, an injunction repeated throughout the five books of Moses. With the exodus from Egypt, around 1250 B.C., the Israelites began to assume the contours of a people. But the defining moment for both Judaism and the Jewish people was the divine revelation at Mount Sinai—a collective experience that impressed on Jews of all subsequent generations that their national and spiritual identities are entwined.

Jews understand the early biblical period as a process of gradual sanctification. First, the people of Israel experience physical freedom, the prerequisite for choosing divine service. Then the Jews receive the Torah at Mount Sinai and learn that there is no freedom without discipline, and that the highest freedom is fulfilling God's will. Then they enter the Holy Land, for which they must be spiritually worthy. Finally, in the tenth century, after 300 years of national consolidation, King Solomon builds the Jerusalem Temple, where Israel can experience God's presence. With the consummation of a dwelling place for God, the land of Israel realizes its sacred potential, its very purpose as the ground where divinity and humanity mingle.

From that high point of sanctity, though, the next millennium is largely an account of spiritual and finally national decline—the latter a consequence of the former. Paradoxically, it was precisely in this period when ancient Judaism reached its most exalted achievement, in the emergence of such great prophets as Isaiah and Jeremiah, who simultaneously castigated Israel for its failings and comforted with their poetic visions of redemption.

THE SYNDROME OF EXILE AND RETURN began in 722 B.C., with the destruction of the secessionist northern kingdom of Israel and the exiling of its ten tribes, leaving the tribes of Judah and Benjamin in the southern kingdom of Judah. The ten tribes vanished into history, becoming the focus of legend and longing, especially among powerless Jews in the Middle Ages, who imagined a mighty army of lost kinsmen emerging from a hidden corner of Africa or Asia to redeem them from their oppressors.

The next wave of exile occurred in 586 B.C., with the Babylonian destruction of the Kingdom of Judah, including the Jerusalem Temple, and the exile of the nation's leaders to Babylon. The exiled Jews were allowed to return 70 years later, and the Temple was rebuilt and a Jewish commonwealth reconstituted. But about 600 years later, the Romans destroyed the Second Temple and what remained of Jewish sovereignty. The symbol of Jewish defiance against Rome became the desert fortress of Masada, where, in A.D. 73, close to a thousand men, women, and children are said to have committed suicide rather than fall into Roman hands. The final Jewish revolt against Roman occupation occurred in 135 and ended in mass Jewish slaughter. Over the next few centuries, most Jews were exiled from the land. The exile persisted until the establishment of the state of Israel in 1948. Still, throughout the period of dispersion, some Jews continued to live in the land, maintaining an unbroken if minority presence as successive waves of conquerors populated the country.

Jews understood the repeated expulsions from the land not as the consequence of military or political defeat but of spiritual defeat, the failure to be worthy of living in a holy land. Exile was fulfillment of the Bible's warning: "You shall therefore keep all My statues, and all My ordinances, and do them, that the land where I bring you to dwell shall not vomit you out." The sojourn of the Jews in the land of Israel is conditional, dependent on their fulfillment of God's commandments, their transformation from an ordinary into a holy people.

Yet built into the Jewish experience is a deep ambivalence. Throughout history Jews have simultaneously longed for holiness and normality, to be chosen and to be like everyone else. One significant moment of confrontation between those opposing worldviews occurred when the elders of Israel approached Samuel the Prophet, who lived about 1050 B.C., and demanded that he anoint a king over Israel. Why, replied Samuel incredulously, would you want to be governed by a king when prophets, direct emissaries from God, govern you? But the elders persisted, and Samuel relented and established Israel's monarchy.

Jews have never resolved that opposing tension, and the debate continues with unabated passion—in our time, between ultra-Orthodox separatists who uphold an absolute Jewish distinctiveness and reject any contact with the non-Jewish world, and "integrationists" who insist Jews must be part of the general culture.

JUDAISM AS WE KNOW IT DEVELOPED largely under conditions of political and military powerlessness. Aside from small Jewish diasporas in Asia, particularly India and China, most Jews lived in Christian and Islamic lands. Throughout the first millennium of this era, Jewish life and learning were centered in the Middle East, especially Iraq, as well as in Muslim Spain—and from the ninth century onward in France and Germany. To varying degrees, Judaism's fellow monotheistic faiths insisted on an inferior, often humiliating status for Jews; under Christian rule, Jews were sometimes subjected to expulsion and massacre.

The Jewish response to Christianity, influenced by historic experience, was overwhelmingly negative. Leading rabbis dismissed Christianity as an impure monotheism, compromised by the concept of the Trinity. Jews were forbidden by rabbinic custom even to enter a church, whose statuary was perceived to be "idolatry." Still, even during the darkest periods of Christian persecution against Jews, there were more nuanced rabbinic voices, like the prominent 14th-century French rabbinic commentator Hameiri, who lauded Christianity's role in bringing the God of Israel to the nations. Rabbinic attitudes toward Islam, which mostly refrained from violent attacks against Jews, were generally more positive. Islam was seen as a pure form of monotheism, and the normative rabbinic approach permitted Jews to enter a mosque. (In recent years, as large parts of Christianity, especially the Catholic Church, have repudiated their anti-Jewish theology, voices have grown within the Jewish community for a reciprocal reevaluation of Christianity.)

Judaism survived its 2,000-year exile through a dual strategy of continuity with the past and adaptability to changing conditions. On the one hand, Judaism maintains an ongoing dialogue with its most ancient ideas and historical events. Indeed, Judaism not only remembers but also reexperiences the past. "In every generation," exhorts the Haggadah, "one is obliged to regard himself as though he himself had actually gone out from Egypt." Jews experience through reenactment: On Succot, the Feast of Tabernacles, they build booths or huts to recall the Israelites' desert wanderings; on Hanukkah, they light menorahs to recall the miracle of the Temple's oil lamp, which had barely enough oil for one night but lasted eight.

At the same time, Judaism has constantly evolved, selectively incorporating new ideas from its host cultures and adapting them to a Jewish worldview. In the Middle Ages, for example, leading Jewish thinkers like Maimonides responded to challenges posed by Muslim thinkers and embraced Greek philosophy. And beginning in the 19th century, large numbers of Jews embraced Western culture, seeking ways to synthesize its insights with Judaism. Crucially, Judaism learned to reorient itself from a faith grounded in its own land, with the Temple at its center, to a faith located everywhere and nowhere, with the synagogue as its capital. Judaism became a kind of portable "citizenship," binding

Jews around the world with a common language of devotion and enabling them to avoid the pressures and temptations of converting into the faiths that dominated them.

The formulator and custodian of the Jewish transition from sovereignty to powerlessness was Rabbinic Judaism (known today as Orthodox Judaism), which developed in the land of Israel in the first centuries of this era and became normative Judaism through the subsequent centuries of exile, its preeminence largely unchallenged until modern times. Rabbinic Judaism is the system of religious observance based on interpretation of biblical law and morality. Rabbinic Judaism divides the Jewish canon into two inseparably interwoven categories—the "written law" and the "oral law." The written law consists of the five books of Moses, the Prophets (covering the period from the entry of the Jewish people into the land of Israel to the destruction of the First Temple), and the Writings (a collection of post-First Temple works like the Books of Ezra and Nehemiah, as well as inspirational works like the Psalms and the Song of Songs).

The oral law is the vast body of legal and moral commentary on the written law, which evolved over centuries through study and debate among rabbis and rabbinic schools. Initially transmitted orally from generation to generation, it was redacted in Israel around A.D. 200 into the Mishnah (meaning "to learn"), a largely legal commentary on the Hebrew Bible. That was followed by the Talmud, between 400 and 500, an extensive commentary on the Mishnah, which is composed of rabbinic arguments over mostly legal issues that are often deliberately left unresolved, on the assumption that "both are the words of the living God." Despite being transformed into written form, the oral law continued to be treated as an evolving tradition based on study and debate, enabling each generation to create its own living relationship with the Jewish canon. Debate became an integral part of the rabbinic system, which taught Jews the value of creative discord. And so even as it imposed conformity of behavior, Rabbinic Judaism encouraged a measure of individualist thinking. Rabbinic Judaism rejected a literalist reading of the Bible, which would have imposed doctrine over creativity. Instead, Rabbinic Judaism focused on centuries of accumulated biblical interpretations—legal, moral, philosophical and mystical—shifting Judaism from a Bible-based to a Talmud-based faith.

The study of Talmud became a central element of Jewish religious practice and identity, and students were encouraged to join the intergenerational rabbinic arguments and offer their own insights. That religious culture of inquiry and literary criticism helped prepare Jews for their eventual entrance into Western culture, and their astonishing success in the arts and sciences.

For Rabbinic Judaism, sacred study is a central act of devotion, almost a form of prayer. Study is a lifelong and ever deepening pursuit; halakah, rabbinic law, emerges from rabbinic study. When Jews invoke sacred study, they speak of "learning Torah." In that context, "Torah" refers to the whole body of sacred writings that include the written law and the oral law, mystical works, religious homilies; in fact, anything at all related to sacred study becomes absorbed in the term "Torah." In its more literal usage, "Torah" refers to the five books of Moses, or to the parchment scroll on which the five books of Moses are written and stored in the synagogue ark.

For all its creativity, Rabbinic Judaism periodically declined into rigidity and nonresponsiveness to the social and spiritual needs of its adherents. At such times, movements of renewal, often mystical in nature, would emerge to reinvigorate the rabbinic system. One such movement was Hasidism, which arose in Eastern Europe in the late 18th century as a revolt against the Talmudic scholasticism that had become increasingly detached from religious devotion. The Hasidic renaissance emphasized joyous prayer and love of God as well as religious study, releasing extraordinary creative energies in inspirational literature and music. Perhaps its greatest achievement was to transform complex kabbalistic concepts into readily accessible ideas and devotions for the Jewish masses.

In the 19th century, as Jews began to leave their self-contained communities and enter Western society, a revolt emerged against Rabbinic Judaism itself, seen by many as an impediment to full Jewish participation in the general culture. The revolt was launched in Germany, with the creation of Reform Judaism, and quickly spread to other Jewish communities in the West. The founders of Reform Judaism substituted morality and prophetic monotheism for the centrality of halakah, insisting that Judaism wholly embrace the spirit of the times. Conservative Judaism, conceived in mid-19th-century Germany, sought to position itself between Reform and Orthodoxy by adopting a generally liberal view of halakah. Orthodoxy itself divided into relative modernists, who accepted some measure of interaction with secular culture, especially secular studies, and ultra-Orthodox antimodernists, who rejected any compromise with modernity. Both wings of Orthodoxy generally continue to deny legitimacy to the Reform and Conservative movements, which Orthodoxy claims violate an unbroken chain of spiritual authority beginning with Moses and extending through Rabbinic Judaism. (The non-Orthodox movements, pluralist by nature, naturally recognize Orthodoxy as a legitimate Jewish stream.)

The place of women in Judaism is a key point of disagreement between Orthodoxy and non-Orthodox denominations. Both Reform and Conservative Judaism grant equality to women in ritual and Jewish law; women are ordained as rabbis, and there is mixed seating in the synagogue. Orthodoxy, by contrast, relegates women to a curtained area in the synagogue and denies them the right to publicly bless the Torah or lead prayers. Yet traditional Judaism did contain progressive elements for its time. The Bible, for example, commands the husband to satisfy his wife sexually. In rabbinic law wife-beaters are punished, and the only criterion for determining whether a woman was raped is the woman's own judgment. The dignity of the woman is emphasized throughout the religious literature and upheld in halakic rulings. In recent years, a growing Orthodox feminist movement has emerged, and is backed by some liberal Orthodox rabbis. The movement sponsors separate prayer services conducted entirely by women, as well as religious academies that are producing a generation of Orthodox women scholars. Orthodox feminists believe that halakah contains sufficient wisdom and legal precedent to be made responsive to the needs of contemporary women; indeed, that responsiveness is one of halakah's great challenges today.

PERHAPS THE CENTRAL IDEOLOGICAL STRUGGLE among Jews in modern times has been an unprecedented attempt to redefine the most basic meaning of Jewish identity. In the last two centuries, several key movements within Jewry tried to separate peoplehood from religion. The Reform movement initially insisted that Judaism was a faith without a nation. On the other end of the spectrum, elements within secular Zionism, founded in the late 19th century, proclaimed the Jews a nation without a faith. Both attempts at radical redefinition of Judaism failed. Today, the Reform movement enthusiastically embraces an identity based on both peoplehood and religion, while the secular state founded by the Zionist movement has incorporated religious values and symbols into its official identity. Individuals may define themselves as either national Jews or religious Jews; but for Judaism itself, nationhood and faith remain inseparable concepts.

By far the most successful modern revolt against Rabbinic Judaism was led by secular Zionism. The founders of Zionism sought to transform passive Jewish longing for a return to the land of Israel into an active program of settlement and state building, and to replace rabbinic authority with a secular leadership. Yet Zionism was not only a radical break with the religious past but also its confirmation—providing a secular structure to fulfill a religious vision. It is precisely that paradox inherent in Zionism that forms the basis for the conflicted identity of the state of Israel—a secular state in a holy land.

Although secularism was the dominant strain within the Zionist movement, it also attracted a strong "modern Orthodox" wing. As the national movement of the Jewish people, Zionism included Marxists and capitalists, territorial maximalists and territorial compromisers, theocrats and anticlericalists. Though united by the ancient vision of a return to Zion, secular and religious Zionism offered opposite interpretations of that dream. Secular Zionism promised that, by creating a modern democratic state and transforming the Jews from a minority everywhere to a majority in their own land, it would "normalize" the Jewish people and turn it into a nation like all other nations—precisely as the elders of Israel demanded of Samuel the prophet. Religious Zionism, though, promised that, by ingathering the exiles into Zion, it would restore the biblical era's intimacy between God and Israel and allow the Jews to finally become a holy nation, which is possible only in the land of Israel.

By promising to fulfill those opposing longings for normality and chosenness, Zionism succeeded in appealing to Jews across ideological boundaries. But it bequeathed those contradictory expectations to the state of Israel, which has become the ideological battleground determining the future of Judaism.

The founding of the secular state of Israel is one of the most momentous religious events in Jewish history. The return of Jewish sovereignty to the land of Israel, with Jerusalem as its capital, has assumed a central place in the Jewish imagination, along with other defining moments of Judaism, like the revelation at Mount Sinai and the destruction of the Jerusalem Temple. Some religious Jews even regard the founding of the state of Israel as the beginning of world redemption—creating an unexpected convergence of messianic expectation with Christian evangelicals, who have become passionate supporters of Israel. Such theological recklessness is perhaps inevitable, given that the Zionist success story fulfilled several of traditional Judaism's prerequisites for the messianic era, including the restoration of Jewish sovereignty in the land of Israel and "the ingathering of the exiles," as Jews call the return to Zion.

The secular founders of the state perceived modern Israel as a repudiation of classical messianism, a revolt against the Jews' passive waiting for the messiah to restore them to the land. Yet Israel's founders were tempted by utopianism, a kind of secular messianism. The socialist Zionists, who founded the kibbutz movement of collectivist farms and who led the state of Israel in its formative years, believed that a socialist Israel would fulfill the prophetic vision of the Jewish people as a "light to the nations," becoming an example of egalitarian justice. In recent decades, as socialist enthusiasm waned, the utopian longings of secular Zionism faded. But those longings reveal how difficult it is to create a purely secular Jewish state.

Contemporary Judaism has scarcely begun to integrate the success of Zionism into its ritual. Partly that's because Judaism, like any faith, incorporates change slowly. But the more compelling reason is that Jews aren't quite sure what to make of this secular state that stirs such profound religious emotions. Probably the majority of Israeli Jews are positioned somewhere between those attributing messianic meaning to the state and those denying it any religious significance at all. Even many non-Orthodox Israelis believe that the resumption of Jewish sovereignty, especially after the Holocaust, is a miracle and proves that God still maintains some form of relationship with the Jewish people; at the same time, many Orthodox Jews agree that the state has no "higher" purpose beyond the vital one of protecting the Jewish people. Most Israelis are pragmatic, in their faith as well as their politics, and are hardly anticipating an imminent redemption. Instead, they continue the long tradition among Jews of irony about the messiah's belated appearance and skepticism about his existence entirely.

For most Jews, religious or secular, Israel's creation after the Holocaust confirms the eternity of the Jewish people. Precisely at the moment when all hope seemed lost, the Jews not only survived but triumphed. Israel became the spiritual solace for the Holocaust, indeed its mirror image: Where the Nazis ingathered the Jews from across Europe into death camps, Zionism ingathered the Jews from around the world into Zion. Jewish faith today veers between those two poles of modern Jewish history. The Holocaust undermines belief in an all-powerful and redemptive God, while the return to Zion seems to reaffirm it. With the realization of the great fantasy of return, Jewish life without the state of Israel has become inconceivable. Arguably for most Jews, the destruction of Israel would destroy the heart of Jewish peoplehood, a blow from which Judaism might not recover.

A religious Jew living in Israel today feels a sense of spiritual completion simply by experiencing daily life. There is constant overlap between his duties as a religious Jew and as a citizen of a modern Jewish state. His religious calendar and his national calendar are identical; Hebrew, the language in which he prays, is also the language in which he works and shops. Serving in the army is a religious act, defending the Jewish people in their land. His very presence in this landscape reassures him that, despite ongoing struggle, the Jewish story is moving on its historical track.

He regards the creation and growth of a thriving Jewish state as a divine gift, and his very identity as an Israeli as a miracle. He considers himself the repository of centuries of prayers, and feels a sense of awe and gratitude for living in this time of fulfillment.

THE INGATHERING OF THE EXILES HAS BROUGHT together immigrants from perhaps a hundred countries, an interracial mini-humanity that uneasily shares the common but not commonly defined identity of Jew. From that bewildering diversity, Israelis have formed four major blocs divided along religious lines.

The first bloc, the "traditionalists," is composed of Jews who observe some form of tradition and are neither strictly Orthodox nor dogmatically secular. About 35 percent of Israelis identify themselves as traditionalists, and probably the majority of them are Sephardim, or Jews of Middle Eastern origin. The Israeli cliché defining this group is that its members attend a synagogue on Sabbath morning and a soccer match on Sabbath afternoon—that is, combining observance and violation of the Sabbath as a seamless whole. Though religiously tolerant in their private lives, many traditionalists vote for the ultra-Orthodox Shas Party, drawn by Shas's militant assertion of Sephardi pride and its resentment of the hegemony in Israeli society of Ashkenazim, or Jews from European backgrounds. The irony, then, is that moderate traditionalists are reinforcing the political power of religious fundamentalists.

The "national religious" bloc, about 12 percent of Israeli society, is Orthodox in observance, strongly nationalist, and generally comfortable in modern, secular Israel. Its young people serve with distinction in the army and combine religious with secular studies. The national religious community is best known for founding the West Bank settlement movement. Though once religiously rationalist, much of the community took a sharp mystical turn after the 1967 Six Day War, which restored the biblical heartland of Judea and Samaria to Israeli rule. National religious theologians have encouraged the first mass outbreak of messianic passion among Jews since the 17th century. In settling Judea and Samaria and restoring "wholeness" to Israel, they say, Jews will restore wholeness to a shattered cosmos. In recent years a moderate backlash within the community has grown, and messianic passion is waning. A strong minority is trying to restore the national religious camp to its traditional political and religious sobriety.

The ultra-Orthodox, who number perhaps 5 percent of the Israeli population, live mostly in their own neighborhoods, a self-imposed isolation from mainstream Israel. Contemporary ultra-Orthodoxy has created the first community in Jewish history where men are expected to devote all their time to studying religious texts, rather than working. The community—which has voluntarily impoverished itself for the sake of Torah study—is largely supported by the wives of full-time religious students and by state subsidies.

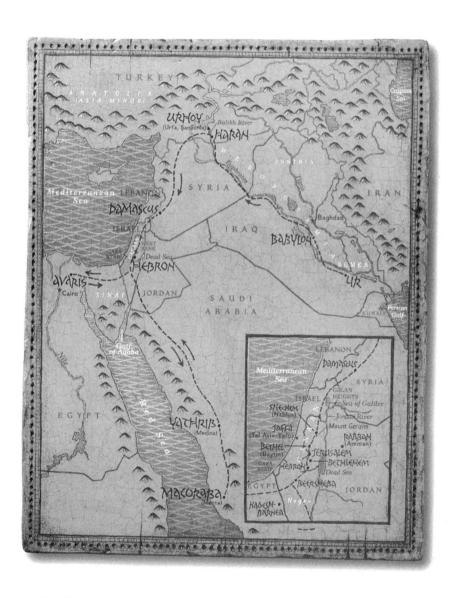

Biblical patriarch of the three great monotheistic faiths, Abraham was born at Ur (map) in present-day Iraq, according to Genesis. As a grown man, he moved with his family northeast, to Harran in today's Turkey. There God instructed him to journey to the Promised Land, where he would found a nation and a people.

The initial justification for focusing an entire community around religious study was to enable ultra-Orthodoxy, shattered in the Holocaust, to restore its spiritual losses. Today, though, the community appears caught by inertia, even as its poverty reaches critical proportions. Ultra-Orthodoxy is deeply ambivalent about its relationship to the state of Israel; half a century after the founding of the state, the ultra-Orthodox haven't recovered from the irony that the great religious dream of return to Zion was fulfilled by a largely secular, even antireligious movement. The ultra-Orthodox support transforming Israel from a democratic into a theocratic state, insisting that only a commitment to Jewish law will prevent the Jews from incurring divine wrath and risking another exile from the land.

Finally, there is the secular bloc, representing nearly half the Jewish population. Only a minority of them define themselves as antireligious. Most observe some form of religious ritual—like the Passover seder or Hanukkah candle lighting—though they tend to interpret those acts as identification with the Jewish people rather than with Judaism. Politically, secularists form the backbone of opposition to religious legislation limiting individual freedom. There is a growing secular backlash against the ultra-Orthodox, whose young men don't serve in the army and whose politicians are adept at manipulating Israel's delicate coalition politics to increase government funding for their separatist communities.

On the fringes of Israeli society, not yet strong enough to constitute a bloc, are the Reform and Conservative movements—dominant among Jews in the West but minuscule here. The non-Orthodox religious movements aren't recognized as valid Judaic streams by the state, which only registers marriages, divorces, and conversions performed by Orthodox rabbis (though it does recognize those acts performed by Reform and Conservative rabbis abroad). That exclusive recognition of the Orthodox rabbinate in matters of personal status dates to the formative years of the state, when there was virtually no non-Orthodox religious presence in Israel. In recent years, Reform and Conservative immigrants from the West have established small communities, but their power has been more than offset by the growing political clout of ultra-Orthodoxy. Still, the Reform and Conservative movements have made some inroads into Israeli consciousness, and the state fully supports schools run by non-Orthodox movements.

THE STATE OF ISRAEL IS A SECULAR DEMOCRACY tempered by religious legislation. The secular founders of the state, seeking domestic harmony with the Orthodox minority and also legitimacy for the new state as a continuation of the Jewish story, attempted to create a compromise between secular and religious expectations. The main concessions to the Orthodox were accepting the Sabbath as the official day of rest, forbidding commerce and public transportation, and entrusting matters of personal status for all Jewish Israelis to Orthodox rabbis. (Parallel arrangements for non-Jewish Israelis were made with clergy of other faiths.)

Depending on the Israeli being asked, the Jewish state is either a stifling theocracy or a hedonistic society mimicking the worst excesses of the West. It is a country where Orthodox rabbis can deny the right of a religious marriage to a "bastard," defined by the Bible as the offspring of a married woman who conceived with another man. And it is the only country in the Middle East with an annual gay pride parade, attracting tens of thousands of participants. In its essence, Israel is a place of paradox, the uneasy meeting point of Jewish nationhood and Jewish faith; its repeated clashes over religion and state form a vital experiment in Jewish redefinition.

In recent years, the relationship between religion and state has come under constant assault. Ultra-Orthodox Israelis want more religious legislation, secular Israelis less. Parliament is a principal arena for redefining the status quo, with religious and secular parties jostling over the identity of the state. The Orthodox parties have expanded their influence—for example, enforcing the suspension of Sabbath flights for the state-owned national airline. At the same time, an increasingly activist Supreme Court has put the brakes on religious legislation. And a popular revolt has led to the widespread opening of restaurants and places of entertainment on the Sabbath. Moreover, increasing numbers of Israelis, refusing to grant the rabbinate power over any aspect of their lives, now fly to Cyprus for civil marriages (recognized by the state when performed abroad). The recent mass immigration of one million Russian immigrants—overwhelmingly secular, many of them intermarried—has substantially boosted the anticlericalist camp, led to an unprecedented rise in pork consumption, and increased domestic pressure for the introduction of civil marriage and divorce within Israel. A major upheaval within Israeli society appears inevitable.

Yet even among the majority of Israelis who support increased separation of religion and state, most acknowledge that total separation is impossible, because of Israel's unique situation as a nation that defines itself, in part, in religious terms. Judaism, a faith that presumes to be relevant to all areas of life, can hardly remain indifferent to the reconstitution of Jewish sovereignty in the land of Israel. Indeed, religion permeates even those issues of identity and politics that aren't strictly "religious." In the debate over the future of the West Bank, for example, both sides cite Jewish tradition: Settlers believe Israel will betray centuries of longing for the land of Israel if it surrenders the biblical heartland, while peace activists believe that Israel will betray the biblical mandate to treat the stranger justly if it insists on annexing the territories.

The long-term struggle of Israeli society is to define the limits of rabbinic influence and especially to reexamine the decision to grant Orthodoxy exclusive right to define Jewish legitimacy. Paradoxically, even as Israel has encouraged the national renewal of the Jewish people, it has stifled a renewal of Judaism by imposing an Orthodox monopoly.

Orthodoxy's claim to preeminence within Judaism is compelling. For 2,000 years, after all, Rabbinic Judaism defined the faith. Yet the upheavals of the last two centuries—including westernization, the Holocaust, and the return to Zion—have been so momentous that most Jews no longer turn to Rabbinic Judaism, which developed under conditions of loss of sovereignty, for answers to their social or spiritual dilemmas. Israeli Orthodoxy tends to be suspicious of the outside world, and sees one of its primary goals as protecting Jews from foreign influences. Theologically, it remains committed to a separatism based on Jewish chosenness. Those are hardly the qualities needed for a people that have regained power and seek their place among the nations in an increasingly interdependent world. Judaism needs to develop new Israeli expressions that address the spiritual requirements of a modern, sovereign people.

The state of Israel, like Judaism itself, is a work in progress. Israel has created unprecedented complications in Jewish self-definition but also offers unprecedented opportunities for Jewish renewal. For the first time in 2,000 years, the Jews can define themselves without a minority's self-consciousness.

Together with the vibrant American Jewish community—the other major center of Jewish life today—Israelis are trying to understand what it means to be a free Jew in a world of intensifying change and to decide which elements of Judaism are expendable and which remain eternal. More than ever before, the future of Judaism will be determined by the meaning Jews invest in the story they've inherited.

At the Praetorium, where Jesus was imprisoned before his crucifixion, a pilgrim bows in prayer. Jerusalem's many Christian shrines draw faithful from around the world.

CHAPTER SEVEN

CHRISTIANITY

AND THE WORD BECAME FLESH

CHARLES M. SENNOTT

TWO THOUSAND YEARS AGO, JESUS OF NAZARETH—OR AS
his fellow Jews would have called him, "Yeshua"—was born into a family of carpenters in a troubled area of the Roman Empire. He would
become, through the centuries, the central figure of Western civilization. Yet, historically, who was he? The four canonical Gospels of Matthew,
Mark, Luke, and John tell his story in the Christian New Testament and
were all written within 75 years of his life. Each of the four authors of these
sacred texts brings his own perspective and understanding to the man.
The cores of their stories coincide, but since the 19th century, biblical
scholars have discussed the many differences among these narratives, raising important questions about the viewpoint of each Gospel and how each
chooses to interpret Jesus' ideas and life in the context of the time in which
he lived.

So how can Jesus best be understood? One way to explore the historical Jesus is by analyzing him in his own context as a Jew living within
a time of diverse social and religious expressions of Judaism. He was one

among a variety of teachers in Judaism, but his disciples understood him as the messenger referred to by the Prophet Isaiah as the Messiah. To the renowned but radical biblical scholar John Dominic Crossan, Jesus was a Jewish peasant, a revolutionary living under Roman occupation, a leader of resistance to oppression through peaceful and nonviolent means. He was a teacher who drew on the teachings of his Jewish faith and on the divine inspiration that Christians believe he held to challenge the land's accepted notions of tribe and family. Crossan sees him as a man truly of the rugged terrain of the Middle East, but one who changed the world around him by daring to question its focus on progeny and land and its often destructive culture of revenge.

There are many other views of Jesus. Some scholars believe he was not a peasant at all but of a more comfortable class of artisans, and that he was most likely a learned rabbinical leader. Others say that the man Christians believe was the Messiah should be seen in the tradition of healers and mystics who traveled the land, preaching folk wisdom. His radical teachings opened up the covenant of Judaism to a universal message intended to enlighten all peoples and all levels of society—rich and poor, Jew and gentile.

During the time in which he lived, the themes that shaped the world around him were the same themes shaking the Middle East today: occupation, religious extremism, and the misguided quest to control sacred space. Jesus had ideas on all of these issues. But the core of his message, theologians agree, was the arrival of the kingdom of God, with a warm spirit of mercy and an unconditional sense of forgiveness. Forgiveness, he insisted even as he was facing death by crucifixion, was the path to reconciliation with one's enemies—an idea that remains as radical and challenging today as it was 2,000 years ago.

THE BIRTH NARRATIVE OF JESUS, as told in the Gospel of Luke, begins in Nazareth. The hamlet lay about ten miles off the Via Maris, the great trade route that linked Damascus with Gaza and Egypt and stretched from the Jordan River to the Mediterranean. Archaeological excavations reveal that the population in Nazareth in the first century A.D. would have been no more than 150 people. Mary, the young girl who would become Jesus' mother, was roughly 15 years old when, Luke recounts, the archangel Gabriel appeared to her. He announced that she would bear a son, whose name would be Jesus, and that he would be "great, Son of the Most High, and the Lord God will give to him the throne of his ancestor David." This miracle of the virgin birth put great strain on the teenage mother and her betrothed, an elderly carpenter named Joseph.

The Nazareth of Mary and Joseph—both probably illiterate Jewish peasants—was a harsh and solitary place overseen by the Romans. In this sense, Nazareth was an occupied village, and its residents lived under the heavy burdens of Roman rule and taxation. According to Luke, when Mary was almost ready to give birth, she and Joseph were called to Bethlehem by the Roman government, to be counted in a census. They set off on the difficult journey of approximately 80 miles and presumably traveled by donkey through the Galilee hills, down the Jordan River Valley, and across the Judean Desert to the small town of Bethlehem. In Bethlehem, Mary and Joseph found no accommodations and resorted to taking shelter in a manger—a cave, where shepherds protected their herds from the elements. It was in this manger—over which the Church of the Nativity was later built—that Mary gave birth to the child.

After the birth, Luke's Gospel continues, an angel appeared in the hills above Bethlehem to a group of local shepherds guarding their flocks at night, and these simple men became the earliest witnesses to the divine light that Christians believe the infant Jesus brought into the world.

According to the Gospel of Matthew, magi, or "wise men," from the East—probably Persia—also came, drawn by a prediction that a baby had been born in Bethlehem who would be king of the Jews. Learning of this, Herod the Great, whom the Romans had made King of Judea, ordered the killing of all infants under the age of two, to safeguard his own power. But before the slaughter, the Gospel records, an angel appeared to Joseph and told him to take flight with the infant and his mother into Egypt.

Eventually, the family returned to Nazareth, where Jesus probably followed in the footsteps of his father and was trained as a carpenter. Some biblical historians believe Joseph may have worked on a huge project rebuilding the nearby fortified Roman city of Sepphoris.

When he was about 30, Jesus was baptized in the Jordan River. He had traveled there to see his cousin, John the Baptist, who had created his own messianic ministry in the desert wilderness, warning that "the time has come!" People came to him to be baptized—or ritually purified—in preparation for the arrival of the Messiah. Today, the terrain that John walked as a nomadic preacher has changed little. The Jordan riverbed is still a chalky expanse of rocks and weeds in most places, windblown and barren except for green rushes that rise from the riverbanks and sway back and forth in the dry breeze. When John and Jesus walked into the river for Jesus' baptism, John saw the Holy Spirit descend on his cousin from above, and he realized that the man Jesus was the promised Messiah.

After his baptism, the Gospels recount that Jesus retreated into the desert wilderness for 40 days. As it was for the Jewish Prophet Moses before him and Islam's Prophet, Muhammad, after him, the desert represented a place of trial and a test of faith, as well as an opportunity to experience a closeness to God. It was in the desert that God revealed himself to all three of the prophets within monotheism. Its harsh, forbidding landscape provoked the meditations on and conversations with God that would become central to the message of Jesus.

Returning to the Galilee region, Jesus began his ministry. Today, in the rolling hills that descend to the Sea of Galilee, you can feel the presence of Jesus and imagine his life here perhaps more than anyplace in the Holy Land. The rocky shoreline, fringed with palms, thorns, and wildflowers, is much the same as it was in his lifetime. Though Jesus may have had an intense confrontation with good and evil in the desert, it was the Galilee region's gentle, fertile landscape that more profoundly influenced the character of his similarly gentle message. It was in the Galilee, as the region around the Sea of Galilee is known, that Jesus began his ministry and befriended the fishermen Andrew, Simon-Peter, and Zebedee, along with Zebedee's sons James and John. In the village of Capernaum, along the northern edge of the lake, Simon-Peter and Andrew were casting nets from the shallows near the shore when Jesus passed by, recognized the brothers as men he had met through John the Baptist, and invited them to follow him in his own ministry.

JESUS' EARLY MINISTRY CENTERED around the parables he told, drawing on the world around him—fishing, the harvesting of wheat, and the blooming of wildflowers—to make his theology feel tangible to the people who surrounded him. He was attracting larger and larger crowds, not only through his teaching but also because he was performing miracles, walking on the waters of the Sea of Galilee, turning water into wine at a wedding, healing lepers and calming the insane, and raising his friend Lazarus from the dead.

It was during the years of his ministry in the Galilee that Jesus laid out the pattern of life for his followers. Speaking to a large crowd gathered on a hillside overlooking the Galilee, he elaborated a heavenly vision for a better life. His words have become known as The Beatitudes: "Blessed are the poor in spirit, for theirs is the kingdom of heaven. Blessed are those who mourn, for they shall be comforted. Blessed are the meek, for they shall inherit the earth. Blessed are those who hunger and thirst for righteousness, for they shall be satisfied...."

These words were more than just soothing promises. They were a message to the poor and the powerless around him that the kingdom of heaven was upon them. They represented a radical expression of ethics, a quest for justice. And the large crowds hearing this message were worrisome to Jewish leaders. Who was this troublemaker in the Galilee?

News had come to Jesus that Herod Antipas, a son of Herod the Great, had beheaded John the Baptist. It was a sign to Jesus of the harsh response meted out to those who challenged the established power. As word spread of his ministry and the power of his healing miracles, he and his disciples increasingly feared Herod Antipas. They avoided large gatherings and traveled in the hills to stay ahead of would-be captors. These worries and a desire to open his ministry to the Gentiles led Jesus north to Phoenicia, to the port of Tyre on the Mediterranean. On their return trip to the Galilee, Jesus and his disciples crossed through Caesaria Philippi, where, Matthew records, Jesus had a vision of his impending death in Jerusalem. From that point on, the biblical narrative points

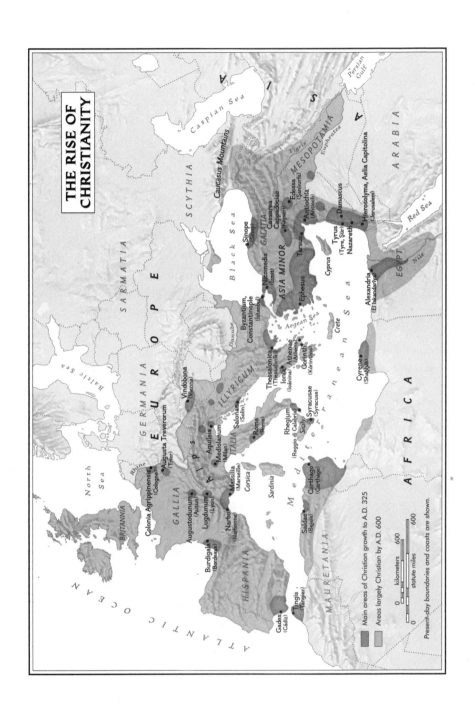

THE RISE OF CHRISTIANITY

Main areas of Christian growth to A.D. 325

Areas largely Christian by A.D. 600

Present-day boundaries and coasts are shown.

0   kilometers   600
0   statute miles   600

Jesus toward preparing himself and his disciples for the day when he would meet his fate on the cross.

On what Christians refer to as Palm Sunday, Jesus rode into Jerusalem on the foal of a donkey—conscious of the resonance this image carried in Jewish tradition of the humble arrival of the Messiah. Luke records that "as he approached Jerusalem and saw the city, he wept over it and said, 'If you, even you, had only known on this day what would bring you peace—but now it is hidden from your eyes.'" He believed that in rejecting him, the city rejected its own salvation. And he warned that someday the city and its great temple would be nothing but ruin.

Below him, the Second Temple of Judaism sent smoke curling up into the sky from its sacrificial fires. Jesus lashed out at what he saw as the misuse of the sacred place, which he felt had been contaminated by commerce. He overturned the tables of the money changers and set free the caged pigeons that were sold for sacrifice. He preached there in the days before Passover, predicting the destruction of the Temple, and was eyed with suspicion by the priests who ran the Temple and who saw his teaching as blasphemous and dangerous.

As Passover arrived, Jesus gathered with his disciples for a "last supper," actually the seder meal that they, like all Jews, were preparing to celebrate. It was the Thursday after they had arrived in Jerusalem when they secretly gathered in an "upper room" in Jerusalem and Jesus spoke of transforming the bread and wine, making his body and blood present through these signs. Whether in hard physical belief or a softer, metaphorical understanding, Christians all over the world hold that at this moment Jesus was offering himself in sacrifice for the salvation of the world. From the beginning of the church, Christians have assembled to repeat and make real this sacrament of breaking bread and drinking wine, the "body" and the "blood" of Christ.

Knowing that the hour of his death was upon him, Jesus retreated from Jerusalem into the Kidron Valley and the Garden of Gethsemane, along the base of the Mount of Olives. It was there that Jesus predicted his loyal disciples would betray him. And it was there that he struggled with his humanity, the fate of pain and suffering that lay ahead for him.

Today, the Garden of Gethsemane is in the care of the Franciscan Custody of the Holy Land, and its ancient olive groves still stand. Biblical historians and archaeologists believe the gnarled roots of these trees date from Jesus' time. There are no churches, no chapels, no museums circumscribing the ground today, no glass partitions separating visitors from the sacred space. There is just earth and roots and trees, ancient and gray and yet still bearing a healthy harvest of olives every year.

After being betrayed and then apprehended in this peaceful garden, Jesus was charged by high priests of the Sanhedrin, the Jewish high court, with blasphemy for his claim that he was the Messiah. Reluctantly, Pontius Pilate, the Roman procurator in the province of Judaea and the only official authorized by Rome to rule on capital punishment cases, sentenced him to death by crucifixion. On Friday, Jesus was beaten by the Roman soldiers who guarded him. A crown of thorns was placed on his head, and he was mocked as the "king of the Jews." In return, he prayed, "Father, forgive them. They know not what they are doing." Shouldering the cross from which he would hang, Jesus carried it through the streets of Jerusalem, finally climbing the steep outcropping of skull-shaped boulders known as Golgotha. And there he was crucified, with common criminals to the left and right of him.

As he was dying, darkness descended over the land and he shouted out, "My God, my God, why hast thou forsaken me?" This lament, this questioning of God is seen by many philosophers as one of the most important moments of Jesus' life as a man: In his expression of uncertainty at why God has chosen this to be his fate, his humanity shines through. But in the end, the Gospels say, his final words are: "Father, into thy hands I commit my spirit."

On the third day after he was crucified, Christians believe that Jesus rose again in fulfillment of the Scriptures and his own promise to his disciples. After his death and burial, Jesus' friend Mary Magdalene returned to his tomb weeping and found that the stone covering the entrance had been rolled away, and the tomb was empty. Jesus appeared to Mary Magdalene and later to the other disciples. Eventually he appeared to them again in the Galilee and bestowed upon his 11 remaining disciples the apostolic mission to bring the message he had given them out into the world, beginning in Jerusalem. He led them as far as Bethany on the Mount of Olives.

"While he blessed them," Luke wrote, "he parted from them, and was carried up into heaven."

THE RESURRECTION FORMS the central core of Christian belief and is celebrated every spring on Easter Sunday. In the Old City of Jerusalem, at the Church of the Holy Sepulchre, Orthodox Christians gather for the lighting of the "holy fires" the day before, Holy Saturday. It is a mystical celebration of the arrival of the light that Christians believe Jesus brought to the world. The tomb in which tradition holds Jesus was buried is sealed shut and then "miraculously" a flame emerges from a corner of the edicule, or empty tomb. Soon that light is passed by votive candles among the crowd packing the church. And suddenly a wave of light spreads out over the church and a loud cheer rises up in celebration of the new life that Jesus brings through salvation. The same light is taken by lantern to Orthodox churches all over Israel, the West Bank, and Gaza.

After Jesus' ascension, the people who formed the movement he started quickly went afoul of the Sadducees, the priestly aristocracy that then controlled the Second Temple in Jerusalem. The movement went underground, and nearly all of the disciples eventually fled the Holy Land. Two who didn't leave—James and Stephen—became martyrs.

One of the most ardent persecutors of the Jesus movement at that time was a Pharisee named Saul. But one day, as he traveled on the road to Damascus, he was visited by God and experienced a dramatic conversion to Christianity. He became known by his Roman name, Paul, and biblical historians often paint him as the force who organized the faith into a religion, supported a theology open to gentiles, and brought its message westward into Europe.

The first followers of Jesus were Jews from the Galilee, and his teachings initially spread through the Jewish community. But the movement began to attract Romans and Greeks also, then Syrians in what is today Syria and Lebanon. Armenian Christians came to Palestine as the first pilgrims in the fourth century and ever since have been an enduring presence in Jerusalem. The faith was planted in the dry, rocky landscape of the desert, in the great monasteries of Egypt, and in the protected, mountain monasteries of the Levant.

In the early centuries of the church, Christianity began increasingly to separate from the Judaism that had rejected Jesus' teachings. Christians claimed the Jewish Scriptures as their own but added to them writings about Jesus and called this the New Covenant. As Christianity and Judaism grew apart, Christians developed an argument against Judaism that later became incorporated into the anti-Semitism of more recent times.

Christianity radiated outward across Europe to Rome, where in the fourth century the Roman emperor Constantine accepted Christianity. By the year A.D. 313, Christianity was recognized as a legal religion of the Roman Empire, and Constantinople (Istanbul) became the seat of Christendom's power in the East.

Although Christianity has flourished in many areas of the world in the 2,000 years since the birth of Jesus, it has generally remained a minority religion in the Holy Land for most of that time. Only for a relatively brief period under the Byzantine Empire, in the fifth and sixth centuries, did Christians represent a slight majority of the population. This demographic status was quickly reversed by the onset of Islam in the seventh century and the massive conversion of Arab Christians, along with pagan and nomadic tribes, to the religion of the Prophet Muhammad.

After the Islamic conquest, Christianity lasted as a solid presence for several centuries, then steadily but almost imperceptibly diminished. In the year 1033, a thousand years after the death of Jesus on the Western calendar, a flood of pilgrims from Europe came to Jerusalem, anticipating the second coming of Jesus. Instead, they found death and famine and a forbidding, earthly Jerusalem ruled by Muslims—nothing like the celestial Jerusalem that Jesus' teachings had envisioned. In 1054 the Eastern and Western churches suffered a schism that has divided them ever since. The disagreement was essentially a theological difference over the Trinity and the true nature of the Son of God. But there was also an important political struggle for power between East and West that formed the backdrop of the doctrinal dispute and intensified the lasting rift.

By the close of the 11th century, the Christian pilgrimage had been transformed into something of a military quest: the Crusades. With internecine warfare in Europe threatening to unravel the Holy Roman Empire, Pope Urban II devised the Crusades in part as a way to unify the

Christian forces of the continent to exert Rome's power. The crusaders carried out bloody assaults on Muslims and Jews (local Christians of the Eastern Orthodox churches also often were not spared), to the shouts of *"Deus vult!"* (God wills this!)

The crusaders spread from what is now Syria and Lebanon down to the Holy Land (the area now defined by Israel, the West Bank, and Gaza). Many of the crusaders stayed, and over the ensuing centuries intermingled, through marriage and concubinage, with local communities. The Greek and Russian Orthodox Churches and the Roman Catholic Church all brought their clerics to serve in the land. Architects came to design the cathedrals that would reflect each church's power, and stonecutters and marble cutters followed to give physical expression to the architectural vision. Many of these artisans, too, stayed on.

THE LAYERING OF THESE IMMIGRANTS through history was so heavy that today it is impossible to determine the precise ethnic origins of the Christians of the Holy Land. Their numbers steadily declined through the tumult and wars and the redrawing of the map of the Middle East in the 20th century. At the end of the second millennium of the faith, the indigenous Christian community of the Holy Land had dwindled to what was, in the language of the Hebrew Bible, a "remnant." According to Ottoman-era census data, the Christian population in 1914 was 24 percent of what we today consider the Middle East, including Israel/Palestine, Egypt, Jordan, Lebanon, Syria, Iraq, and Turkey. In the year 2000, the Christian presence in the Middle East was no more than 5 percent and is still diminishing steadily. In the Holy Land the decline is even more precipitous. Church estimates placed the Christian presence at as much as 20 percent in the early 1900s; today it is about 1.5 percent. Some experts studying the situation predict that at the current rate of decline the indigenous Christian presence in Israel, the West Bank, and Gaza could virtually disappear within two generations.

During the time the Ottomans ruled the Middle East, Christians, Jews, and Muslims lived together in relative peace. When the European powers occupied the Middle East after the First World War, they allied with Christian communities, putting these communities at odds with their

Jewish and Muslim neighbors. Today, the diminishing Christian presence in the Middle East rouses little sympathy from the Muslim or Jewish populations, who remember how their ancestors suffered historically at Christian hands, particularly during the Crusades and the Holocaust of World War II. Both of those events still resonate in the land, shaping its politics and the emotions that fuel the recurring cycles of violence. On Fridays, when Muslims gather for the noon prayer, Islamic clerics will often rail about the Christian Crusades and the ancient clash of civilizations that many in the Middle East feel is playing out again today.

As violence once more wracks the area, many of the remaining Christians in Israel are fleeing, emigrating to Europe or America. Not since 1948, when the Palestinian refugee crisis first began for Muslims and Christians alike, has there been what Bethlehem University's Bernard Sabella describes as "an historic flight of Christians."

As it has been since the very beginning of the faith, Christianity in the Middle East is diverse, encompassing Palestinians, Egyptians, Jordanians, Iraqis, and Syrians. Historically, the largest number of Christians here have been followers of the Eastern Orthodox churches, with some following their own national and liturgical traditions. Yet they all share in a tradition that emerged from the Byzantine Empire, with common cultural and historical roots to Greece. The second largest group in the Holy Land—roughly one-third—are members of the Roman Catholic Church (or, as it's often called in this part of the world, the Latin Church). The so-called Uniate churches—the Maronites, concentrated in Lebanon, and the Melkites, concentrated in the Galilee, also acknowledge the primacy of Rome but have maintained liturgies and rituals distinct from those of Roman Catholicism. In addition to these denominations are small numbers of indigenous Lutherans, Anglicans, and Baptists. Very few Arab Christians identify with evangelical churches because the American evangelical movement has backed Israel, and indigenous Christians have suffered under the Israeli policies of occupation and settlement building that the American Christian right supports.

All of these manifestations of Christianity make for an ornate tapestry. But sadly, deep divisions, especially the bitter, thousand-year-old schism between Orthodoxy and Catholicism, too often have torn at this fabric of Christianity, contributing even further to its diminution.

The Greek Orthodox, the Armenian Orthodox, and the Roman Catholic Franciscan Order are the three leading religious entities that share control—almost always contentiously—of the Christian holy sites associated with Jesus' life—the Basilica of the Annunciation in Nazareth; the Church of the Nativity in Bethlehem; the rival baptism sites along the Jordan River; the Via Dolorosa in Jerusalem's Old City, where Jesus carried the cross; and the Holy Sepulchre, where Christians believe he died, was buried, and rose again. Disagreement among the Christian groups over these sites is legendary, and perhaps the only thing that keeps their bickering from turning to violence is a mid-19th-century Ottoman decree known as the Status Quo Ante. It spells out the rules and processional rites and even assigned duties for cleaning and repairing the churches for each of the three groups.

The local Christians, especially those raised as Greek Orthodox, have long been alienated and often openly contemptuous of their church leadership, which is seated in the Patriarchate of Jerusalem. Historically, the patriarchate has not permitted indigenous Christians to serve as bishops or in the highest levels of the church, and the Greek hierarchy has been bitterly accused by Palestinians of selling off church land to Israel.

These disputes are as old as the faith itself—in some ways, they have defined the faith. For when Christians themselves have ruled the Holy Land, they have done so through conquering forces from the West—forces that ironically cared little for the indigenous Christian population, hardly distinguishing it from followers of the vanquished faiths. As a result, Christian rule has often been looked upon very unfavorably by the local Christians themselves.

Christianity, like Judaism and Islam, is rooted in the desert wilderness and in the ferment and violence of the Middle East. And yet it has never really flourished in the land where it began. Today, Christians of the Holy Land are an almost invisible minority, alienated from their own clerical hierarchy and ruled by foreign governments.

In the spring of 2002, the precarious position of Christianity here was laid bare. On the morning of April 2, Israeli forces moved into Bethlehem to root out an "infrastructure of terrorism" in the Palestinian Authority.

Fleeing the advancing force, members of rogue Palestinian militias fled toward the Church of the Nativity, shot the lock off the door of the Franciscan compound there, and forced their way in. Other Palestinian police forces and some civilians also fled to the church for refuge along with dozens of priests, nuns, and monks who live and work in the church compound. Israeli forces ringed the church with tanks and set up robotic sniper rifles on industrial cranes looming over the compound, so they could shoot into it.

At the end of the 37-day siege, there was a solemn procession back into the church as the faith communities reclaimed their holy site. Bullet casings and spent tear gas canisters littered the ancient cobblestones before the entryway of the basilica. As the priests entered the church under the low lintel of the "door of humility," the Franciscans sang a hymn in Latin, and an Armenian monk ritually swung the chains of a censer. The smell of holy incense wafted in the air and mingled with the faint smell of gunpowder and urine and sweat that remained from the people who had been holed up inside the basilica during the long siege. A frail Franciscan emerged from the damp darkness of the church, squinting into the midday sun as the ordeal came to an end. He was thin and unshaven. A 23-year-old Israeli Arab who preferred to call himself a Palestinian, Raphael Tayim said that he had remained in the church because he felt it was his duty as a Christian, that it was part of the sacred role of Christians in the Holy Land to try to stop the two sides of this conflict from killing each other. "We were all praying every day that it would end. I was praying for my life," he said.

Eight people were shot and killed by Israeli snipers during the siege. Windows were shot out all around the perimeter of the building, and a statue of the Virgin Mary was nicked with gunfire. An Armenian monk was also badly wounded, and a blaze broke out that gutted the Franciscan parish center. But the Franciscan was hopeful.

"I think in the end our presence and our prayers saved both sides from even more killing, from turning the church into a bloodbath," said Tayim. "I think there is something mystical in that. Even if our presence here is fading, I think the siege showed just how important it is that we hold on. The priests and nuns and all of us who stayed in our church and refused to let the church become a battlefield were trying to bring the teaching of Jesus, the lessons of nonviolence and forgiveness, into all this. I don't know if anyone heard the message, but I hope they did."

During the annual hajj, thousands of pilgrims gather at the Sacred Mosque in Mecca, fulfilling a main tenet of Islam to visit the holy city at least once in a lifetime.

CHAPTER EIGHT

ISLAM
THE WORD OF THE PROPHET

MILTON VIORST

LEGEND HOLDS THAT THE ARABS AS A PEOPLE ARE DESCENDED from Ishmael, elder son of the Prophet Abraham. To satisfy the jealousy of Sarah, Abraham's wife, Ishmael and his mother, Hagar, were said to have been driven into the desert. In time they made their way to Mecca, a market town in Arabia. There, Ishmael, with his father, Abraham, is supposed to have built the foundations for the Kaaba, a shrine that became holy to the surrounding desert tribes, and later to Muslims.

The Prophet Muhammad, founder of Islam, was born in Mecca in A.D. 570. The faith he gave impetus to now numbers a billion believers, in societies as diverse as Nigeria and Afghanistan, Indonesia and the Maldives. Yet the Arab world remains its heartland and Mecca its hub.

The Arabian desert, never hospitable, was a particularly grim place at the time of Muhammad's birth. Decades of war between two great empires, Christian Byzantium and Zoroastrian Persia, had isolated the desert tribes from their markets to the north. A sudden population surge had strained food and water resources to the breaking point. The discipline of Bedouin life, the traditional key to survival, was fracturing.

Muhammad was a Hashim, a family since celebrated for the dynasty he created. The Hashimites belonged to Mecca's preeminent trading tribe, the Quraysh, who had come in from the desert generations before. An orphan at six, Muhammad was raised by kindly relatives. Though his roots were embedded in the culture of the desert, he was a town dweller all his life.

Little is known of Muhammad's childhood. Mecca, already famous for the Kaaba, was not just a commercial town but a religious center, where pilgrims came to venerate pagan spirits. In the market Muhammad was no doubt exposed to a variety of peoples, Jews and Christians as well as pagans, and at the shrine he heard a range of religious ideas. Still, it was a bleak place for a boy to be brought up. A poet of that era said of Mecca, "no waters flow ... not a blade of grass on which to rest the eye ... only merchants dwell there."

Muhammad was surely a bright child. The legend that portrays him as illiterate was probably fabricated to refute those who maintained that the divine voice he later claimed to hear was actually his own. Trained as a trader, Muhammad is likely to have learned at least enough reading, writing, and arithmetic to serve a trader's needs.

By the time he reached maturity, the mutual exhaustion of Byzantium and Persia had yielded a truce, permitting a resumption of caravan traffic. Merchants were again exchanging products in the marketplace, spices and leathers from the south for cloth and grain from the north. If, as historians say, great changes transpire not when societies are in the depths but when they are on the rise, then it can be said that Arabia was poised for a new experience.

At the age of 25, Muhammad was hired to take command of a caravan journeying to Damascus. Its cargo belonged to a wealthy merchant's widow, who had become prominent in commerce on her own. Her name was Khadija, and Muhammad's biographers write that, on his return, she was so smitten by him that she proposed they marry.

Khadija brought not only wealth to Muhammad but social standing. It is commonly held that she was 40, 15 years his senior, when they wed, but she bore him seven children, which seems to belie such a calculation.

The couple's three sons died in infancy; their four daughters survived to adulthood. Tradition holds that, until her death after 24 years, the two enjoyed a happy, monogamous relationship.

Islamic historians say Muhammad was about 40 when, meditating alone on a hilltop, he received a revelation from God. In Muhammad's mind, he was the same God as the one the Jews and Christians worshiped. Muhammad confided his communications to Khadija, who encouraged him to continue them. Subsequent messages led him to call on Meccans to give up their array of pagan deities in favor of this one, omnipotent God. Though Khadija became a convert, few followed her, and for a decade the community rejected Muhammad, and even harassed him for his heresy.

Muslims are certain the voice Muhammad heard was that of God himself. Muhammad's practice was to commit the words to memory, then impart them to scribes, who wrote them on parchment or palm leaves. Historians regard the pattern, in a culture that was overwhelmingly oral, as plausible. These words now make up the Koran, the compendium of Muhammad's revelations. Muslims believe that they are God's words, verbatim.

Not surprisingly, outsiders have always treated this belief skeptically. During centuries of rivalry with Christianity, churchmen and kings challenged Muhammad's veracity. Though he may truly have heard a voice, say secular scholars, there is no evidence that it was God's. To Muslims, however, these words establish for eternity the special relationship between Muhammad and God.

It is this relationship that distinguishes Islam from other religions. "There is no god but God," the Koran says, "and Muhammad is his Prophet." This rigorous assertion of monotheism is a direct challenge to the era's paganism, but it is more. Muhammad maintained that he was a simple man, unaware of why God had chosen him as divine messenger. He was more like Moses than Christ in acknowledging his own mortality, denying any capacity to perform miracles. Muslim belief describes him as the last in the line of prophets that began with Abraham. Yet the Koran makes clear Muhammad had a unique bond with the divine.

"Believe in God and His messenger," the Koran says. Its verses attribute to Muhammad authority that is all but equal to God's. "Obey God," it says, "and obey His apostle if you would be true believers." From

Islam's earliest days believers followed this commandment, shaping a faith based heavily on the Prophet's words.

During his lifetime, Muhammad proved equal to high responsibility. Having begun as an ordinary merchant, he fulfilled the duties of God's messenger. In time, he served as the head of Arabia's community of believers. Later, he took charge of a government and organized a powerful army. As military commander he conquered Arabia, and as a political chief he laid the foundation for an empire that remains largely intact today.

On the religious plane, Muhammad's initial vision was limited to weaning the merchants of Mecca from idolatry. Later, he enlarged his ministry to include conversion of the desert tribes. Several centuries after his death, when Muslims confronted the challenge of transforming a desert faith into an imperial religion, they turned to him again, seeing in Muhammad, as a paragon among mortals, the model for all believers to emulate.

Muhammad's messages from God, historians agree, took place over a span of some 20 years. Though non-Muslim scholars search for clues to whether the messages changed, Muslims hold that they are all of equal value. Some scholars see indications that his work was not finished, that more revelations were to come, but the faithful regard inquiry into the Koran's divine integrity to be heresy.

Yet even Muslim authorities acknowledge the haphazard way in which the Koran was organized. One of Muhammad's scribes is said to have recorded God's words to the Prophet on a camel's shoulder blade. Not until nearly a century after Muhammad's death did Muslim authorities reach agreement on the Koran's text. The basic unit became a verse called a sura, of which there are 114 in all, each regarded as a separate revelation. Though Islamic scholars agree generally on the sequence in which they were received, they are published in order of length, so that the first revelations, the briefest, appear at the book's end.

THE KORAN IS AN AUSTERE DOCUMENT, reflecting the desert culture from which it emerged. Meant as a sequel to the Bible, it contains some biblical references, but it is without the human dramas that are familiar to Bible readers. Similarly, it is short on history, providing few clues to the nature of the times. In our own age, many of its words and its references are obscure, even to scholars. Much of the Koran consists of divine admonitions directed at everyday life. If there is a theme, it is that life's real meaning lies not on Earth but in the eternal afterlife.

"Recognize," says the text in a summary sura, "that the life of this world is indulgence in delusion, idle talk, pageantry, boasting and rivalry over flaunted wealth and offspring.... But by and by, vegetation dries up, turns yellow before your eyes and becomes straw. That is how it is with the vanities of this life, which is all illusion. But in the hereafter, there is also grievous punishment, and God's forgiveness."

Until a century or so ago, while Muslims read the Koran worshipfully, non-Muslims treated it mockingly. Then the nature of Western scholarship changed, producing experts who studied religion as an intellectual discipline. Though their studies are often derided by believers as "orientalism," they produced much of what is known today of Islam's history, leading to a deeper understanding of Islam both as a civilization and as a faith.

Modern scholars, for example, see in the Koran's references to commerce a sign of Muhammad's own hand. "It is no sin," a sura says, "that you seek the bounty of your lord by trading." Over the centuries, this verse has assured businessmen that they can be holy without compromising their efforts in the marketplace. Many experts have read it as a sales pitch by Muhammad to the merchants of Mecca, a way of luring them into worshiping God.

Some specialists also see signs of Muhammad's morality in Islam's well-known ban on alcohol and gambling. Poets of Muhammad's era have left to us tales of rampant drunkenness and gambling, a threat to desert society. Early Koranic suras urge moderation in these practices, but the excesses obviously continued. Finally, the Koran says, "Strong drink and games of chance and idols... are only an infamy of Satan's handiwork. Avoid them!" Once a priority of the Prophet, the ban has remained intact ever since.

Looking at Arabia's history, specialists point out that monotheism, the Koran's dominant message, was not unknown at the time. Suras refer to Arabia's Jewish and Christian tribes as "people of the book," meaning the Bible. In cryptic form, the suras even refer to biblical stories.

Muhammad, knowing only Arabic, certainly never read "the book," but he may have heard the stories in the course of business. They affirm, say the specialists, Islam's Judaic and Christian roots.

In fact, evidence suggests that Muhammad founded a new faith only because the Jews of Arabia refused to recognize him as God's messenger. A decade of preaching in Mecca had yielded few converts. Khadija was by now dead, and Muhammad needed a different approach. In the marketplace he heard of ongoing tribal disputes in Yathrib, an oasis 250 miles to the north. Muhammad converted some of the merchants he met and, a year later, made a momentous journey to Yathrib to mediate among the bickering pagan and Jewish tribes.

In the summer of 622, Muhammad and 70 of his followers slipped quietly out of Mecca, a few at a time, to avoid alerting their foes. A few days later they reassembled in Yathrib. Their migration—known to history as the *hijra* (Hegira)—-is regarded as Islam's watershed. Yathrib would henceforth be known as Medina, the City of the Prophet. The hijra, which begins the Islamic calendar, would be regarded as the founding point of Islam.

In Medina, Muhammad for the first time took his message beyond the Quraysh, his own tribe. Reasoning that the Jews would be particularly open to his message, he was clearly disappointed to learn that they were quite satisfied with the monotheism that they already practiced. Failing to convert them, Muhammad initiated a bloody war, ultimately driving the Jews out of Arabia.

The pagan tribes he encountered were more amenable to him and agreed to join his community of believers, known as the *umma*. Within a loose confederation, over which he ruled, Muhammad kept tribal autonomy intact. His followers grumbled about his strictness, but they apparently recognized his rules as a way to reverse the decline of desert society. The arrangement also placed hundreds, perhaps thousands, of warriors at his disposal. Muhammad decided to use them to spread the faith by war.

Muhammad's initial strategy was to send out raiding parties against vulnerable caravans, with the aim of obtaining more soldiers and more booty to finance further military action. His victories also brought increasing numbers of converts into the umma. In 623 he targeted a Quraysh caravan coming from Syria, laden with riches. By now a gifted commander, he fell on his old townsmen at the oasis of Badr in 624 and won decisively. The battle is regarded as a turning point in Islamic history.

The skills Muhammad demonstrated were political as well as military. He negotiated a series of political marriages—Muslim historians count nine, well beyond the Koranic limit of four—which added to the tribes under his wing. In addition, he bought with money the loyalty of many tribesmen. Within a few years of the hijra, Muhammad had collected an array of allies and an army of some 10,000 men. They made his community Arabia's dominant power.

Mecca, Muhammad's native city, was his last major obstacle, and by the time he attacked in 630, it was barely able to resist. He arrived home in triumph, swept away the idols, and converted the remaining Quraysh to the new faith. He transformed the Kaaba from a pagan into an Islamic shrine. From his modest beginnings, he was now the chief of a community with a clear political and religious vision. The victory at Mecca opened the way to projecting this vision beyond Arabia to every point of the compass.

But in 632, two years after capturing Mecca and a decade after the hijra, Muhammad died. His successors put down an uprising of some disaffected tribes that aimed to loosen Muhammad's social controls. By then a Muslim raiding party had attacked a Christian town near the Dead Sea. A military momentum had been established, and Muhammad's successors did not hesitate to see it as a way to carry the faith to the heart of the infidel empires of Byzantium in the west and Persia in the east.

HISTORIANS TODAY DEBATE THE INSPIRATION behind the Arab conquests. Bedouin tribes, hard-pressed to sustain themselves, had often conducted raids beyond Arabia's borders. Colonies of Arabs, attracted by greener pastures, had built settlements under the Byzantine and Persian flags. Historians speculate whether the tribes were motivated more by the growing rigors of desert life than by the summons of their faith. A Syrian poet of a millennium ago gives a clue to what drove them on.

No, not for Paradise did thou the nomad life forsake,
Rather, it was thy yearning after bread and dates.

Some scholars say it was easier for the Muslim leadership to divert the restive tribes to conquest abroad than to keep them, lacking in food, under discipline at home.

The Muslims were good soldiers and competently led, fighting enemies, whether Byzantine or Persian, that were often superior in numbers but low in morale. The tribes already inside the enemy homeland helped them. The Muslim forces moved quickly across the landscape on horses and camels, winning many victories through tactical surprise. But their conquests, it is clear, were as much a product of their enemies' weakness as their own strength.

Barely a decade after Muhammad's death, the entire Fertile Crescent was in Muslim hands. Damascus had been seized from the Christians and Byzantium was under siege. Muslim armies had captured Egypt and were moving across North Africa toward Spain. In the east, Persia's capital, Ctesiphon, along with much of its heartland, fell, and the Muslims were fixing their sights on India and Central Asia.

Historians agree that as occupiers the Arabs were generally benevolent. Rather than force Islam upon the defeated, they adopted incentives, such as granting lower taxes to converts. They rarely quartered troops in captured cities. Instead, they built military towns—Kufa and Basra in Iraq, Fustat in Egypt, Qayrawan in Tunisia—that in time became great centers of Arab culture.

But whatever their tactics, the Muslim armies transformed the region from the Atlantic Ocean to the Persian Gulf. Wherever they went, they imparted Arabia's language and its culture, and in time virtually all of the people they conquered, whatever their roots, came to describe themselves as Arabs. No less important, they gave the region the religion—Islam, literally, "those who submit" to God—that defines it to this day.

Indeed, Muhammad's bequest to the Arabs was a faith, a civilization, and a huge territorial patrimony, the Arab world today. Muhammad's personality still lies at the foundation of this phenomenon. Fourteen hundred years after his death, the force of his personality continues to be felt. It is, in fact, the core of Islamic civilization.

In the years after Muhammad's death, Islam's conquests largely over-shadowed the serious conflicts taking place within the Prophet's umma. The trouble began with Muhammad's succession, for which no provision had been made. According to desert tradition, succession was deter-mined by a *shura*, a meeting of tribal chiefs—a concept that was later incor-porated into the Koran. But politics reared its head, and Muhammad's own family objected to this.

Muhammad's closest associates met in a shura and chose as caliph—a term meaning "successor to the Prophet"—Abu Bakr, his dearest friend. The three caliphs who followed Abu Bakr were similarly selected, and the four, exalted for their piety, are known collectively by Muslims as *rashidun*, the "rightly guided." But in fact, the era was as marked by profligacy and conflict as by piety. Though three of the four died by assassination, they left behind the legend that their three-decade reign was Islam's golden age.

Throughout the three decades, an angry opposition led by Muhammad's family challenged the shura's authority. Its own candidate was Ali, who, as cousin and son-in-law, was Muhammad's closest descendant. As the fam-ily saw it, the shura was a conspiracy of old cronies, and they argued that only by limiting the caliphate to the Prophet's kin could its integrity be pre-served. The shura did indeed choose Ali as the fourth caliph, but by then its authority had largely collapsed. The Umayyads, a rival clan, contested his election and ignited a civil war, in which Ali was killed.

The Umayyads, in effect, conducted a coup d'état, using the shura as a facade to claim legitimacy for their own caliphate. Ali's survivors retal-iated by forming a dissident faction. The schism divided Islam into two groups, a majority now known as Sunnis, meaning "people of the faith," and a minority known as Shiites, for "contesting party." The Sunnis remained loyal to the shura. The Umayyads, the Islamic mainstream, complicated loyalties by being usurpers. However reluctantly, most Muslims preferred them to the Shiite rebels.

The Umayyads moved the Muslim capital to Damascus, leaving Arabia as the backwater that it was before the Prophet's time. Their later victory in Iraq over a Shiite army ended the prospect of Shiite dominance, but it did not restore their own good name. Even though the Umayyads preserved Sunni preeminence in the struggle, many Sunnis maintained a grudge and aspired to replace them.

The Umayyads reigned in Damascus for 90 years. Among the reasons they fell was the never solved problem of succession, pitting brother against brother in struggles for power. The Muslim tribes, meanwhile, could not be persuaded to abandon their habits of internecine warfare, thus weakening the regime. As much as anything, however, most Muslims seemed to yearn to restore Islamic legitimacy.

The Abbasids, who brought the Umayyads down, were a family from Muhammad's tribe. From their base in Iraq, they assembled a coalition composed of both Sunnis and Shiites. But a more important source of their power were "new" Muslims, recent converts, most of them from Persia. Muslim legend holds that the Abbasids brought the Umayyads' impious ways to an end, which surely is not true. What they did was to infuse the Arabs' desert culture with ancient Persia's worldliness, softening—at least for a time— Islam's austere nature.

But outwardly the Abbasids were devout, which helped them to conquer. They established their capital in Baghdad, near the heart of Shiite power in Persia, where they recited prayers and built mosques. The Abbasids even made pilgrimages to Mecca. But they also practiced a level of self-indulgence that went far beyond Umayyad practices.

They erected great palaces along the Tigris River, with spacious reception chambers lit by huge chandeliers. They set aside luxurious apartments, which royal concubines shared with eunuch servants. They were served by slaves, wore the finest fabrics and furs, and adorned themselves with jewels. They bathed their bodies with scent and colored their hair. They amused themselves with horse and camel races, and with the performances of professional actors and singers. They dined on gold and silver plates, and dismissed Koranic strictures by getting drunk on wine.

At their apogee from the late eighth to the mid-ninth century, the Abbasids also brought grandeur to Arab culture. Their empire was the world's most powerful and Baghdad the most dazzling city, known everywhere for its wealth and commerce, its scholarship and arts. Harun al-Rashid, the most eminent Abbasid caliph, exchanged letters with the Frankish king Charlemagne, whose small realm still languished in the Middle Ages. The famous gift that Harun sent Charlemagne, a brass water clock, was technologically superior to anything the West had ever produced.

Harun's son al-Ma'mun became caliph in 813 and is remembered for his lavish tastes. He was married, it is said, on a golden mat studded with sapphires, while minions showered him and his bride with pearls. But al-Ma'mun, whose power base was heavily Shiite, is also noteworthy for his efforts to reunite Shiite Islam with Sunni Islam. Unprecedentedly, he named a Shiite as heir apparent, and gave him his daughter in marriage. But the Sunni masses were mortified by the prospect of a Shiite caliph, and the action, far from unifying Islam, brought the empire to the brink of civil war. Al-Ma'mun's retreat ended the last serious effort to repair the breach between Sunni and Shiite.

No less important was the impetus al-Ma'mun gave to reexamining Islam. Since ancient times, the manuscripts of Greek thinkers had been stored in Byzantine cities. The Abbasids, in the course of their conquests, acquired an appetite for them and established in Baghdad a school of translators and interpreters who, in a few decades, absorbed what the Greeks had taken centuries to produce. Harun's preference was texts in medicine and astronomy; al-Ma'mun went further to seek out the works of the great philosopher Aristotle.

A tenth-century chronicler recounts that al-Ma'mun once asked Aristotle in a dream "What is beauty?" and was told, "That which is beautiful to our reason." The legend reveals how Hellenist the Abbasids had become. It also suggests a society close to embracing intellectual values that promised to lead Islam far from its desert origins.

The age of the Abbasids, infused with influence from the Greeks and the Persians, unleashed in fact a huge surge of intellectual creativity never duplicated within Islamic civilization. Arabs contributed grandly to mathematics and astronomy, to medicine and geography. Arab architecture excelled. The Arabic tongue, hitherto limited to the Koran and popular poetry, suddenly became the language of literature, used by intellectuals throughout the Mediterranean region.

In this atmosphere, a school of theologians known as Mutazilites initiated a challenge to religious orthodoxy. Its objective was to imbue Sunni Islam with the principle of rational inquiry. It also promoted a belief in free will, at odds with the orthodox doctrine of divine predestination. Mutazilites were not freethinkers; they professed an awe of God and the Koran. But they rejected the arid traditionalism that tribal culture had imparted to the faith. They aimed to replace it by a search for understanding of divine will through human reason.

The Mutazilite outlook, however, never won popular support. At least part of the reason was the Abbasids' alienation from the pious masses, who resented their extravagance, their wine drinking, their sexual conduct. Al-Ma'mun's flirtation with the Shiites had also widened the breach with these masses who, notwithstanding Baghdad's wealth, were a deeply impoverished underclass. Too conservative to be tempted by Greek thought, they were nostalgic for the old-fashioned life of shared austerity.

Orthodox theologians fought vigorously against Mutazilism and its values. They argued that human reason was at best a faulty instrument, unsuited to ascertaining God's will. Indifferent to the sciences, they maintained that the Greeks presumed to elevate human powers to the level of God's. They pronounced the doctrine of free will an attack on divine omnipotence. They declared Mutazilism to be heresy, and, in a contest that sometimes degenerated into physical violence, the masses supported them.

By the time al-Ma'mun died in 833, Greek thought was in disarray. Mutazilism endured vestigially for another century or two, far from Islam's main current, but the Arab world's era of intellectual audacity was over. It had become a victim of a triumphant conventional wisdom.

Ironically, the liberal ideas cultivated by the Arabs during this era, along with the texts at their source, gravitated westward, to Italy and to Spain, to become the germ of scholasticism, then of the Renaissance, from which emerged modern Western civilization. Islamic civilization, meanwhile, walked away from the embrace of reason, a fateful decision that has narrowed its nature ever since.

IT WAS ORTHODOX THINKERS, after Mutazilism's fall, who placed a permanent stamp on Islam. The Mutazilites had argued that believers should establish a personal bond with God, based on reason. Orthodoxy held that the faith had to bind the entire community and be defined by laws rooted in inherited traditions. Since the Prophet's time, orthodox thinkers had argued endlessly over what the true traditions were. The Mutazilite threat persuaded them of the need to resolve their differences.

Muhammad ibn Idris al-Shafi is recognized as the leader of the school of scholars that brought the sharia—the legal system—to completion. Though born in the seaport town of Gaza, he was, like Muhammad, raised in Mecca, where he imbibed the culture of the neighboring Bedouin. Al-Shafi arrived in Baghdad in 803 and became a teacher of classical "traditionism," the craft of establishing the traditions, or precedents, according to which Muslims were to live.

Al-Shafi could not be called original, much less innovative, terms that most Muslims would in any case consider disparaging. He dismissed reason as insignificant in the quest for understanding and regarded the Greek inspiration of his Mutazilite adversaries as a stain on Islam. Nonetheless, al-Shafi, with ingenuity, imparted a new orientation to Islamic thought, laying the foundation of the sharia that has since endured.

Islamic scholars were, of course, of a single mind on the primacy of the Koran as the source of Islamic law, but they acknowledged its failure to cover the spectrum of life's contingencies. All accepted the centrality of tradition as a backup. But when neither the Koran nor known tradition provided a guide, where could believers turn? Al-Shafi turned to the Koran's command "Obey God and the Prophet." God, he contended, meant this command not just for Muhammad's lifetime but for eternity.

Islamic scholars prior to al-Shafi had rejected the Prophet as the overriding repository of law on the grounds that he was too human, and thus fallible. Al-Shafi persuaded them with the argument that the powers God conveyed to Muhammad were so vast, and his wisdom so great, that he outranked all other sources of authority.

Al-Shafi went further to contend that in setting a precedent—called a *hadith,* or "tradition," in Arabic—the Prophet overruled the words of God himself. Though this claim at first upset the diverse schools of traditionists, within a few years the so-called *sunna* ("way") of the Prophet had been adopted, side by side with the Koran, as the foundation of Muslim jurisprudence.

Having erected the scaffolding, al-Shafi left it to others to lay the sharia's bricks. From all over the Arab world, believers volunteered to seek out hadith, the individual sayings and acts attributed to Muhammad. Curious as it may seem, for the remainder of the ninth century, these volunteers engaged in a frenetic search that produced some 600,000 samples of Prophetic words and deeds, which became the raw material of Islamic law.

The seekers of hadith were not so much jurists as legal reporters, who made voyages of discovery to every Muslim community. Some were very serious about their work; for others it was a kind of sport. In the competitive atmosphere that the process engendered, most researchers emphasized quantity. Such, obviously, was the prestige of being privy to segments of the Prophet's life that seekers were often tempted to embellish, if not to lie.

Even among Muslims, the process produced wide skepticism. Muhammad, after all, had died two centuries before the search began. This meant that any of his sayings or acts would have had to pass through at least a half dozen intermediaries before falling on a researcher's ear. Aware of the risks, al-Shafi's disciples worked at establishing authenticity. Though they never managed to inoculate the system from error, at least one Western expert concluded that, whatever the flaws, as a body the hadith reflected the values of the era. They are, he argued, what the Prophet would have said or done.

Al-Shafi's disciples devised a sliding scale of credibility as a warning and guide to later generations. But they nonetheless declared the hadith to be judicially binding. At the beginning of the tenth century, they embarked on deliberations to shape them, in all their diversity, into a comprehensive body of divine law.

These deliberations—known as *ijtihad*, from jihad, which means "personal struggle"—were designed to end in scholarly consensus of what the law was. Once such a consensus was reached, the decision had no appeal. Each law that was adopted, considered equal in authority to the Koran, was said to be divine. Within a few decades the scholars had examined all the hadith, published their work in dozens of manuals, and declared the law to be complete. By that they meant that it was complete for all time, and that Muslims had the duty to accept it without questioning.

Every Muslim knows the expression "The door to ijtihad is closed." It refers to the orthodox concept that no modification of Islamic law is permitted, however the times might change. Not every Muslim accepts the concept as valid. Shiites, while accepting the sharia, consider ijtihad open, at least on some issues. But in Sunni Islam, the orthodox view has largely prevailed, and over the past thousand years little beyond ornamentation has been added to the tenets written by al-Shafi's school. It has made the sharia a sturdy barrier to change in Islamic life.

The sharia blankets Islamic life. The Prophet's precedents apply not only to grand concepts but to trivialities such as social manners, forms of greeting, and items of dress. They inform a believer not only what his religious duties are and what makes him ritually clean or unclean but what he can eat or drink, how he should dress and treat his family, and generally what he may with good conscience regard as permissible acts. Obviously, not all Muslims follow its dictates literally. Nonetheless, true believers regard the sharia as a guide to all of life, as "the whole duty of man."

Al-Shafi and his disciples, in shaping this law, linked the Prophet Muhammad with the faithful in an almost corporeal way. Far from creating an organic law, sensitive to changing conditions, they based the duties of Muslims on life in seventh-century Arabia. As such, the law appeals particularly to the superorthodox, the fundamentalists, who regard this moment in time in a narrow corner of the Earth as Islam's golden age. But other Muslims lament that, after al-Shafi, the brilliance of Arab civilization, demonstrated in Baghdad in the tenth century, was forever extinguished. Al-Shafi and his apostles, they say, crushed Islam's creativity, replacing it with the rigid concept of obedience to authority that governs Arab society today.

For nearly a millennium after the completion of the sharia, Islam flowed on like a great river, its bed undisturbed, its course unswerving.

Muslims were bound by the sharia to the Five Pillars of faith, accepted by Sunnis and Shiites alike. At their heart is the profession of faith: "There is no god but God, and Muhammad is his messenger." The other duties are prayer five times a day, the giving of alms (zakat), the observance of the Ramadan fast, and a pilgrimage (hajj) at least once to the holy cities of Mecca and Medina. Orthodoxy obviously imposed other duties: Men are limited to four wives, women must dress modestly, both must desist from drink. It also banned bi'da, doctrinal innovation.

Christianity, historically, was equally averse to innovation. But in these same centuries it was shaken by the Copernican revolution, riven by the Protestant Reformation, forced to adapt to the secular assaults of the Enlightenment. These were tumultuous times, during which the West constantly remade itself. Not so for Islam.

Arabs waged war against other Arabs, and then fell to the Ottomans, but Islamic culture made few connections with the outside world. A few major thinkers emerged—the philosopher Ibn Sina (known in the West as Avicenna, 980–1037) and the sociologist Ibn Khaldun (1332–1406), for example—but they received more attention in the West than at home. Muslims met Christians in battle during the Crusades and during the Ottoman campaigns in Europe. But they kept clear of foreign ideas, which helped to ensure the immobility of their civilization.

Sufism, long a dissident school, emerged in the centuries after al-Shafi, seeming to take a different approach. In reaction to orthodoxy's rigorous ritualism and legalism, it offered a personal, emotional, mystical Islam. But its teachings were not so much an alternative as a complementary channel to the divine. Though it endured, it did not transform Islam's standard practice or belief.

Far greater was the impact of the fundamentalist crusade of Muhammad ibn 'Abd al-Wahhab in Arabia in the 18th century. His ideology, known as Wahhabism, far exceeded the Prophet's in austerity. Wahhabism was intolerant, even xenophobic, and starkly puritan, allowing no singing, dancing, or smoking. It found a vehicle in the House of Saud, which used it as a weapon in extending the family's dominance over the peninsula. Much of the wealth the Sauds obtained later from oil went into spreading Wahhabism among Muslims everywhere.

NOT UNTIL NAPOLEON APPEARED OFF EGYPT'S COAST in 1798 did the Arab world have to deal with a threat to its values from the Christian West. Napoleon's army easily occupied Egypt, hub of Islamic culture, erasing any doubts about the West's technical and organizational superiority. Within a century, almost all of the Arab world had been absorbed into Western empires.

This trauma inspired young Muslims to learn Western languages and enroll in Western universities; many Arab states adjusted their institutions and laws to emulate European practice. Yet, at the start of the 20th century, the sturdy foundations of Islamic culture remained intact. Equally important, the society was falling still further behind in its age-old rivalry with Christianity.

That was when Muhammad 'Abduh, an Egyptian theologian, challenged Arabs to adopt a new outlook to confront the West. Both pious and nationalist, 'Abduh saw that Islam could no longer afford to ignore Western values. But being a religious man, he was not prepared to concede a central point: that the West's power was probably a product of the secular nature it had been forging since the Renaissance.

'Abduh considered secularism—the measure of good and evil on a human scale—a derogation of God. Islamic society, he believed, must and could catch up with the West, but without sacrificing its religious character. A thinker rather than an organizer, 'Abduh promoted a theology that evolved into the movement known as modernist Islam.

'Abduh blamed Islam's failure on orthodoxy's tenacious grip on the society. Departing from the conventional view that Islam was already perfect, he maintained that Muslims had much to learn from the West. Western ideas and methods could be adopted selectively, he argued, enriching Muslim life without adulterating its religiosity. He reproached the orthodox elite for intellectual lethargy, and proposed that it peel away what he considered the layers of spurious doctrine that for a millennium had burdened Islam. He called for Muslims to open the door to ijtihad and bring reason into Islamic law and Islamic life.

'Abduh was convinced that his Arab nationalism, widely popular in the imperialist age, would win the masses to religious reform. But the masses were not swayed. Like their ancestors, who centuries before had supported orthodoxy against Greek thought, they showed little interest in 'Abduh's newfangled concepts. Orthodoxy regarded 'Abduh as a heretic, and the masses agreed.

Islamic modernism succeeded in sinking roots among Arabs only in the realm of the late King Hussein. The king was scion of a dynasty, the Hashimites, that had long been rivals of the Sauds. Foes of Wahhabism, the Hashimites reigned in Mecca until the Sauds drove them out in the

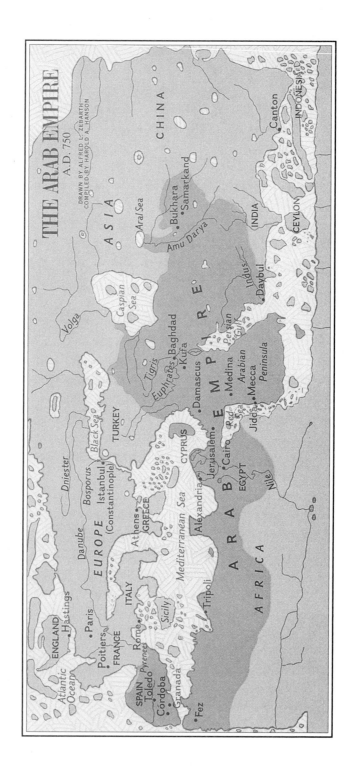

THE ARAB EMPIRE
A.D. 750

DRAWN BY ALFRED L. ZEBARTH
COMPILED BY HAROLD A. HANSON

1920s and, with British help, they settled in Jordan. During his lifetime, King Hussein argued for reopening ijtihad, for reexamining the Koran's meaning, for encouraging innovation in the faith. He promoted democracy and women's rights, but, with few resources, he failed to spread his view of Islam beyond Jordan's borders.

After a century, modernist Islam remains a movement of a small minority. Its following is chiefly among Westernized intellectuals, many of them living abroad. Though the Muslim masses are aware of their backwardness relative to the West, they have never been persuaded that modernist reforms would reward them, either in this life or the next. They have responded, in fact, far more warmly to the call of fundamentalism, a doctrine at the opposite end of the religious spectrum.

Fundamentalism as a popular movement started as a protest against Turkey's decision to depart from the Islamic consensus after World War I. The Turks had come late to Islam. A Central Asian people with linguistic links to Mongolia, they were converted to Sunni orthodoxy after migrating to the Middle East in the 11th century. In 1453 their principal tribe, the Ottomans, seized Constantinople, putting an end to the Byzantine Empire. Within a half century their armies had conquered virtually all of the Arab patrimony. In 1517 they declared that their leader, the Ottoman sultan, would henceforth occupy the 1,300-year-old caliphate, making them the highest power in Islam.

But even as the dominant force in the Middle East, the Ottomans steadily retreated before the growing strength of Christian Europe. Severely wounded by Napoleon, the Ottomans experimented with Western methods, but they failed to forestall collapse in World War I, and from the ruins of their empire Kemal Atatürk rose to leadership.

Atatürk, a wartime general, became a revolutionary political leader. He proclaimed Turkey a democracy and proceeded to rebuild the society along Western lines. He also abolished the caliphate, declaring Turkey a secular state. In the ensuing decades, his vision has guided Turkey's struggle to become modern. But the Arabs, first as Western colonies and later as independent countries, showed no disposition to follow his model. Most Arabs, in fact, consider Atatürk an apostate. The popular outrage toward Turkish secularism, and especially the caliphate's end, fueled fundamentalism's rise in the Arab world.

Many Muslims, it is clear, saw the disarray of their world and accepted a need for change. Their institutions were enfeebled by long identification with the corrupt regimes that had flourished under the Ottomans. 'Abduh's modernism, moreover, had cast doubt on old traditions. But rather than blame their decline on a failure to absorb the teachings of the West, many Muslims attributed it instead to a waning popular dedication to Islam's eternal values.

Hasan al-Banna, a charismatic schoolteacher from the town of Isma 'iliya in the Nile Delta, gave a new structure to Islamic fundamentalism in the 1920s, when he founded the Muslim Brotherhood. Its objective, he said, was to establish an Islamic state, modeled on seventh-century Arabia, free of the secularism that had been imposed by colonialism and the corrupted institutions of orthodoxy. Al-Banna's movement, unlike 'Abduh's, was activist from the start. He declared that every Muslim's duty was to strive—to make jihad—for the triumph of Islam. Though he never talked of it openly, violence was from the beginning intrinsic to the Muslim Brotherhood's message.

Al-Banna's message was two-pronged. It rode the vehicle of anti-colonial xenophobia but it also promoted a return to Islam's mythical golden age, the era of the rashidun. Both had strong popular appeal, among the middle as well as the poorer classes. Within a few years of its founding, the Brotherhood had tens of thousands of supporters in every Egyptian province, while its adherents numbered in the millions throughout the Arab world.

Fundamentalism, as al-Banna presented it, had a huge advantage over ideologies like democracy and socialism. It tapped into a system of belief that had been around for 1,300 years. Muslims were clearly comfortable with the legends of the rashidun, just as they were relaxed in old mosques. Unlike Judaism and Christianity, Islam never had to reach an accommodation with secular ideas. This meant that, in times of trouble, Muslims reverted instinctively to religious remedies. When the masses were offered fundamentalism, they were already familiar with it.

In Egypt in the 1930s and 1940s the Brotherhood focused on murdering colonial officials and the Egyptians who worked for them. After the killing of an Egyptian prime minister in 1948, the authorities retaliated by murdering al-Banna himself. But even after Gamal Abdel Nasser in

1952 overthrew Egypt's depraved king and abolished the remnants of colonialism, the Brotherhood's violence did not stop. The Brothers considered Nasser's regime, being secular, as sinful as its predecessor.

A young Egyptian named Sayyid Qutb became al-Banna's intellectual heir, and he revised the doctrine of Islamic warfare for the postcolonial age. Nasser's Egypt was pagan, he said, like Arabian society prior to the Prophet. Nasser, he insisted, was no better than Atatürk. Qutb argued that Muhammad himself had legitimized violence in waging war against Arabia's Jews and pagans. From this he concluded that faithful Muslims must not shrink even from murder to build an Islamic state.

It would be inaccurate to suggest that most Muslims have come under the influence of Qutb, or even al-Banna. Most, in fact, are content to live peacefully in states that fall far short of the Islamic perfection of which the extremists dream. Only a small fraction of the Middle East's Muslims, moreover, look to violence to solve social problems. Recognizing as much, many fundamentalists call themselves democrats, insisting their goal is to establish an Islamic state only by popular consent.

Still, a hard core proclaim that Islam demands warfare until victory. They claim to serve God by forcing Islamic practice on believers, and by killing apostates. Their social vision, of a present-day umma ruled by the sharia, is much like orthodoxy's. In their commitment to violence, however, they are the heirs of al-Banna, the founder of the Muslim Brotherhood, and of Qutb, his apostle.

Nasser had Qutb hanged in 1966, and Egypt's orthodox theologians dutifully proscribed his writings, but his influence spread throughout the Arab world. In 1981 assassins claiming guidance from Qutb's works declared Egypt's President Anwar Sadat, Nasser's successor, a pagan and they gunned him down. Though the chief culprits were tried and executed, extremism was clearly on the rise.

This extremism was given momentum by the Islamic revolution in Iran in 1979. Led by Ayatollah Ruhollah Khomeini, Iranians overthrew the secular government of the pro-Western shah and established a state run by Shiite clerics. In proclaiming an Islamic republic, guided by religious law, the revolutionaries provided a precedent to Islamic extremists everywhere. Their great contribution was to show it could be done. But Persian culture was different from Arab culture, and Shiites were different from Sunnis. As a result, Khomeini's state was quite different from what Sunni extremists had envisaged.

Since the time of Ali, the fourth caliph, Shiites had gone off in their own theological direction. They never accepted the caliphate. Persuaded that a successor to Ali would arise, they oriented their beliefs toward a golden future, in contrast to the Sunni ideal of reverting to a lost past. They did not regard sharia as unchangeable and encouraged ijtihad, reexamination. They admitted rationalism into their debate and kept an open door to innovation. Khomeini's institutions, though authoritarian, were uniquely Shiite, far from the model of the rashidun. More important, they were not regarded as fixed forever.

Not surprisingly, within a few years after Khomeini's death in 1989, a movement for reform began asserting itself. Khomeini's clerical followers fought tenaciously to retain their powers, but a popular wave led by younger, liberal clerics demanded more democracy, a more accountable government, and greater personal freedom. The reformers also demanded more contact with the secular West, and they won election to important offices. Though it held on, the Islamic state was seriously undermined, making clear that in Iran Islamic extremism was in decline.

That was by no means true in the Sunni world, however.

Observers of Islam shifted their attention from Khomeini to Osama bin Laden, a Sunni extremist. Bin Laden's roots were in the Wahhabism of his native Saudi Arabia; the doctrine of violence that he embraced clearly came from the work of Sayyid Qutb. What he also brought to his ideology was a grasp of Western organization and technology. Bin Laden put his beliefs into action in destroying the World Trade Center towers in New York and attacking the Pentagon in Washington on September 11, 2001. The horror of this action triggered a war in which Islam was at the center. Bin Laden imperiled not only the West but, in the eyes of many Muslims, the Islamic world as well.

Bin Laden's objective was to discourage Muslims from reaching any accommodation whatever with modern times. Strategically, he sought to suppress by every means within his power what he regarded as the evils of Western society.

The signs that have come from Islamic society since the New York atrocity are that a small minority of Muslims, but not more, are willing to follow bin Laden. His action puts Islam's worst face on display. What Islamic society has not shown, after centuries of stagnation, is a capacity to rebuild itself in a manner relevant to the times. If many Muslims despair of becoming modern and find an attractive alternative in bin Laden's fundamentalist vision, others recognize that Islam must establish a constructive relationship with the 21st century. In response to this challenge, only Muslims themselves can decide the course that Islamic civilization will take.

INDEX

PUBLISHED BY THE NATIONAL GEOGRAPHIC SOCIETY
1145 17th Street N.W., Washington, D.C. 20036

Printed in U.S.A.

Library of Congress Cataloging-in-Publication Data

Cradle & crucible : history and faith in the Middle East /
introduction by Daniel Schorr ; with David Fromkin ... [et al.].
p. cm.
ISBN 0-7922-6597-1 Softcover
1. Middle East--History. 2. Middle East--Religion. I. Title: Cradle and crucible. II Fromkin, David.
DS44 .C73 2002
956--dc21
2002033800

Cradle & crucible

PUBLISHED BY THE
NATIONAL GEOGRAPHIC SOCIETY

John M. Fahey, Jr., *President and Chief Executive Officer*

Gilbert M. Grosvenor, *Chairman of the Board*

Nina D. Hoffman, *Executive Vice President*

PREPARED BY THE BOOK DIVISION

Kevin Mulroy, *Vice President and Editor-in-Chief*

Charles Kogod, *Illustrations Director*

Marianne R. Koszorus, *Design Director*

STAFF FOR THIS BOOK

K. M. Kostyal, *Editor*

Rebecca Lescaze, *Text Editor*

Melissa Farris, *Designer*

Patrick Booz, *Researcher*

Carl Mehler, *Director of Maps*

Joseph F. Ochlak, *Map Researcher and Editor*

Matt Chwastyk, Gregory Ugiansky, *Map Production*

Gary Colbert, *Production Director*

Ric Wain, *Production Project Manager*

Sharon Kocsis Berry, *Illustrations Assistant*

Michele Callaghan, Judy Klein, Molly Roberts, Melissa Ryan, *Consulting Editors*

Arzin Amin, *Research Assistant*

MANUFACTURING AND QUALITY CONTROL

Christopher A. Liedel, *Chief Financial Officer*

Phillip L. Schlosser, *Managing Director*

John T. Dunn, *Technical Director*

Vincent P. Ryan, *Manager*

Clifton M. Brown, *Manager*

Alan Kerr, *Manager*

PICTURE CREDITS

Cover Ed Kashi; vi, Alexandra Avakian; viii, Alexandra Avakian; xvi, Courtesy Ghazi Bisheh, Ministry of Tourism and Antiquities, The Hashemite Kingdom of Jordan/Photograph by John Tsantess,Smithsonian Institution; 18, Reza; 44, Reza; 66, Courtesy The Library of Congress; 78, Agence France-Presse/Fayez Nureldine; 95, NG Maps; 102, Reza; 123, Art by Marc Burckhardt, Calligraphy by Julian Waters; 128, Annie Griffiths Belt; 144, Mehmet Biber